Self Defense Everyone Should Know

NEAL MARTIN

NEAL MARTIN

Copyright © 2013 Neal Martin

All rights reserved.

ISBN: 1490455116
ISBN-13: 9781490455112

DEDICATION

To my Dad for all his help and guidance over the years.

CONTENTS

	Acknowledgments	i
	Introduction	1
1	Take Responsibility	4
2	Make A Gameplan	8
3	Awareness (Or Take A Look Around Once In A while)	12
4	Learn To Communicate	18
5	Know Yourself	24
6	Learn To Manage Fear And Adrenaline	34
7	Learn Situational Control Skills	46
8	Get Fit	53
9	Do Combatives Training	55
10	Learn To Hit Hard	62
11	Tap Your Aggression	74
12	Learn To Hit First When Necessary	80
13	Self Defence And The Law	87
	Appendix A: Violent Intent And Instilling Panic	93
	Appendix B: Cultivating A Presence Of Mind To Counter-Balance Fear	99

Appendix C: Some Things You Should Know About Real Fighting	105
Recommended Resources	108
About The Author	109

ACKNOWLEDGMENTS

My thanks goes out to all the martial arts teachers and self defence instructors that I have trained with over the years. A special thanks to my father, who is also my Jujitsu sensei, for all the training, guidance and support he has given me over the years. Thanks also to Geoff Thompson for the inspiration, and to Mick Coup for helping me keep things real. An extra special thanks also goes out to the students at On Guard Gym for sticking with me and putting up with the pain!
Extra special thanks is reserved for my wife Wendy, without whose love and support I couldn't do what I do, and for my other three special girls, whom I live for.

INTRODUCTION

"Self defence is not about learning a whole bunch of cool physical tricks. Self defence is an attitude that is backed up by a few very simple practical strategies and tactics. There are no guarantees and it is as much about acknowledging your limitations as it is about developing your strengths." **Neal Martin**

There is a lot of bad information out there on self defence. Look around YouTube and the myriad blogs and websites that exist on the web and what you will find are an awful lot of people who proclaim to know all about good self defence, but in fact haven't got a clue what they are talking about most of the time, and indeed the information they are putting across to people could potentially do more harm than good.

If you are new to self defence and have never done any kind of training before then it can it seem that most of the fighting systems and arts out there look really effective for self defence. A quick trawl through YouTube will reveal countless videos of people teaching what appear to be really cool and useful moves that could work against a real attacker.

The truth about most of these cool moves is that they are little more than neat little physical tricks, like magic tricks designed to wow spectators and people who don't know any different.

And most people *don't* know any different. To know what works and what is really useful in a physical confrontation requires one to have some kind of experience in these things (or to have at least trained with other people who have). Most people don't have that experience because most right thinking people tend to avoid violence like the plague.

Others, like me, actively sought out violent situations in order to know them better and to find out the best ways of dealing with them. I went into the bouncing game for precisely that reason. I wanted experience and I wanted to see what worked. And what I found was, the vast majority of the information being taught as self defence simply had no bearing whatsoever on real life.

You see, self defence is not about learning a whole bunch of cool physical tricks. Self defence is an attitude that is backed up by a few very simple practical strategies and tactics. There are no guarantees and it is as much about acknowledging your limitations as it is about developing your strengths.

This book will not teach you how to do all those physical tricks beloved of martial artists and self defence practitioners the (web) world over. Instead this book will give you something far more valuable. It will give you a sound game plan and the tools to help you develop the right attitude which will not only help you take responsibility for your personal safety, but also help you prevail in any conflict situation.

The information I have chosen to include in this book is designed to be of real practical value. There is next to no theory in it. I want to give you information that you can use right away to formulate your own self protection game plan, information that is going to help you prepare yourself mentally and physically should you ever have to defend yourself in a conflict situation.

All the information in here is taken from my thirty odd years of experience in the martial arts and self defence worlds, and also the practical experience I gained from working doors for many years.

Read each chapter and let the information sink in. Let it colour your developing attitude towards your own personal safety. To stand any chance of developing a good game plan you have to start thinking in a certain way. At points in the book I will explicitly explain this attitude. At other times you will have to read between the lines for yourself.

I have no doubt that by the time you are finished this book you will be far better equipped to protect yourself and your loved ones than what you were in the beginning, as long that is, as you put what I tell you into practice. Even if you don't, you will still find a change in attitude, and sometimes, that's all it takes.

So let's crack on and take a look at some self defence fundamentals first of all, beginning with the most important thing: how to take responsibility for your own personal safety.

1 TAKE RESPONSIBILITY

"I don't even call it violence when it's in self defense; I call it intelligence." **Malcolm X**

Making a full commitment to taking responsibility for your own personal safety is paramount when it comes to self defence.

One of the main barriers to personal safety that many people have in today's society is that they believe they have no need for any kind of self defence skills or general self protection game plan.

There is no doubt that there is much violence in the world and that it is never far away from our own doorstep. If you watch the news or read the newspapers on a regular basis you would be forgiven for thinking that our society is more violent than it actually is. Even though there is much violence in today's society, the times in which we live are actually not as dangerous and violent as many believe they are, despite the impression that the mainstream media puts across. As hard as it is to believe, the levels of criminal violence in our society are less than what they were in recent years and beyond. Yes, there is still much violence out there, but not as much as people generally believe.

I'm reminded of the late great comedian and social commentator, Bill Hicks, talking on stage about the news media and how it paints a vivid picture of this truly frightening and horrible world filled with death, violence, war, famine, destruction, disease etc. on a daily basis. And then you look out your window and...nothing, just the sound of silence or crickets chirping in the background. To quote Bill: *"Where is all this shit happening?!"*

My point here is that the world is not as horrible and

violent as some would have you believe. Lots of self defence instructors out there have a vested interest in making people believe that the world is a scary place, that you could get mugged or raped or killed at any time.

While this may be true to an extent, the world is nowhere near as bad as these unscrupulous instructors would have you believe. That's just marketing, scare tactics to try and get people to sign up to their classes and expensive courses, nothing more.

So am I saying that the world in which we live is some kind of peaceful paradise where violence and street crime don't exist? Of course not. Obviously these things exist. What I'm saying is that you need to maintain a healthy psychological attitude towards all the bad in the world. Acknowledge that it exists, but at the same time don't let it affect your life in any adverse way. Don't allow fear or paranoia stop you from living your life to the full.

At the same time, it would be foolish to think that violence will never cross your path. The risk of violent confrontation still exists, yet many people choose to deny this fact, and therefore don't see the need for any kind of self defence training.

Some of the reasons people overlook self defence training are:

- A fear of the unknown (don't like to try new things)
- They possess a defeatist or negative attitude - I can't do it!
- They think the police will protect them- they won't!
- They live a very sheltered lifestyle, walking around with a "it can't happen to me" attitude.
- They think it requires too much effort—laziness, in other words!
- They are naive or oblivious to the real world.
- They believe God will protect them.

- They claim they don't have the time or are too busy to look into self defence training.

When looked at, none of the above reasons hold any water. The most important reason from that list to reconsider is the fact that some people think the law or other people in general will save them if anything happens to them.

No! The law will not save you. Why would you think the police are going to be there if something happens? Have you ever called the police out anyway? How long did they take to respond? Exactly.

Only you can take responsibility for your own personal safety, and it is something that you *absolutely* must do. You must have the attitude that if something happens, no one will be there to save you, so you have to learn how to save yourself.

There is terrific strength to be gained from making this mental shift. No one likes to feel reliant on anyone else. There is nothing worse.

Becoming self-reliant, especially in regard to your personal safety, will not only give you an increased sense of confidence, but more importantly, should you find yourself in a situation where you must defend yourself or risk injury or death, you will react swiftly and forcefully, because you know that it is up to you to do so, that no one will magically appear to save your ass.

You have to save your own ass!

I really can't stress enough how important this is: take responsibility before you do anything else. Everything else you do in regards to self defence must come from that initial decision.

By committing to taking responsibility for your own personal safety you are also making a secondary commitment, which is this:

That you will never be anybody's victim.

You must tell yourself that you have the inalienable right to live your life in peace and that no one has the right to threaten that peace in anyway. If someone does threaten you in a physical manner then it is your duty to stand up for yourself and defend against any physical violence that comes your way.

If you don't install this belief from the start then you will never be sure about your actions in a self defence situation. You are drawing a line in the sand, knowing full well that if anyone crosses it you will react swiftly and forcefully to drive them back over it again.

We will go more into this subject later on in the book.

In the meantime, take a look at the practice drill suggestion below. There will be suggested practice drills in each chapter of this book and they are designed to help you focus and give you action steps that will greatly improve your self protection skills. Once you read a chapter, try out the practice drill. It is essential that you do more than just read about things, you must apply the advice I give you in some practical way, otherwise you will be no better equipped to defend yourself than you were when you first began reading this book.

Practice Drill

Sit down and think about what your personal safety means to you and how far you are willing to go to protect yourself and your loved ones. Think about the fact that you can't rely on anyone to save you if you are in trouble, and then make the firm decision that you will take full responsibility for your own safety from now on. Keep reminding yourself of this decision daily until the belief is firmly ingrained in your mind.

2 MAKE A GAMEPLAN

"Every fighter has to go in there with a game plan." **Rau'Shee Warren**

When it comes to your personal safety it is useful to have some kind of game plan in place, a set of instructions if you will, that will help you get through a situation, in this case, a physical altercation.

Going blind into any kind of difficult situation is not the best plan of attack. After all, you wouldn't climb into the boxing ring to fight and just hope for the best. You would already have figured out what your approach to the fight is going to be, how you are going to fight and what to do if things go a certain way.

Self defence is no different. You need to plan ahead and decide what steps you are going to follow should you find yourself in a situation where someone is being hostile or violent towards you.

Having a game plan in place will give you the biggest chance of success and of handling the situation in the right way. You can't be thinking about what you are going to do while the situation is unfolding. It's too late then, and you won't be able to think clearly because of the massive stress you'll be under.

What you need is a self protection game plan put in place. A basic set of instructions that you can follow in most sets of circumstances.

In one sense, this whole book is a self protection game plan, just a very detailed one. In this chapter however, I want to give you an overview of what a good self-protection game plan should be all about. Then in the succeeding chapters, I'll go into more detail on the various aspects of that game plan. So let's look at the overview first.

Awareness And Target Hardening

Awareness should be bedrock of your self-protection gam plan. After all, it is by being aware and "switched on" to your environment that you can avoid most trouble in the first place. Awareness makes it possible for you to spot trouble from afar or sense impending danger. The quicker you pick up on that danger, the more options you will have to deal with it and avoid it altogether. Your options become severely narrowed when trouble is right on top of you. We'll discuss awareness in further detail in the next chapter.

Target hardening is a term that simply refers to making yourself a less easy target for criminals and those who would wish you harm. It's about how you present yourself to the world, how you carry yourself, how you interact with other people and the signals you put out to other people, especially those that may be after their next victim, like street predators. Again, we'll discuss in more detail later.

Avoidance And Escape

It should be your goal to avoid trouble as much as possible, to keep yourself out of situations that may pose a danger to you.

Should you find yourself in trouble then your main priority should be to escape the situation wherever possible. There is no merit in staying in a dangerous or life threatening situation if you don't have too, unless of course you have no choice. Sometimes you just can't escape or you must stay to protect third parties, such as a loved one.

Situational Control And Verbal De-escalation

If you find yourself trapped in a situation and all

avenues of escape are temporarily blocked then you must begin to take control of the situation as much as possible. If faced by a would-be assailant then you need to use your contact management skills to control your personal space and make it difficult for the other person or persons to attack you.

At this stage of the game, your priority should be to try and talk the other person down, to verbally de-escalate the situation. Many times, if you are confident and assertive enough, you can defuse a situation without recourse to physical violence. More on this later.

Pre-Emptive Action

Sometimes, no matter what you do or say, a situation cannot be defused by verbal de-escalation and it will quickly become clear (through your aggressors actions and body language) that an attack is imminent. In this case, your best course of action is pre-emptive action, i.e. you hit your attacker first before they hit you. This may sound like a brutal or even thuggish course of action, but believe me, it is almost always the best course of action and it will nip the situation in the bud before it escalates any further.

Don't worry if you can't see yourself doing this. Later in the book I will show you exactly how you can get the right mindset that will allow you to take pre-emptive action whenever necessary.

The plan here is to hit and run whenever possible. You should always be thinking about escaping the situation at the earliest opportunity. Hitting your attacker will give you that opportunity, buying you time to make your escape.

That in a nutshell is a basic self-protection game plan. In a high stress situation like a physical altercation you

won't have time to think too much, that's just the way it is. The more prepared you are, the more options you will give yourself and thus the greater your chances of prevailing in an attack situation.

Now, in the remaining chapters of this book, I'm going

to go into a bit more detail about the concepts and principles laid out in this game plan, plus a whole lot more.

Let's do this!

3 AWARENESS (OR TAKE A LOOK AROUND ONCE IN A WHILE)

"Situational awareness is a cumulative alertness to threats, environment, movement and anomalies. Those anomalies are called pre-incident indicators, the visually unlikely circumstances that collectively indicate an attack could be imminent. Being adept at quickly determining threat potential — without looking like you're about to implode — is invaluable on the street." **Kelly McCann**

It has become a bit of a cliché in self defence circles to say that awareness is the bedrock of good self defence; that self defence starts with awareness. Every self-protection instructor in the world now pays glib homage to this statement whenever they teach people (especially newcomers), before moving swiftly on the really cool physical stuff that everybody pays their money for.

I don't mean to suggest here that the concept of awareness in self defence isn't an important one. It is, obviously. It is very important.

There is usually a problem though, in the way that awareness is taught, if indeed you could be said to be teaching awareness. For the most part awareness isn't taught, it's merely relayed to students in the manner of a lecture, which usually means dry and boring. You generally don't take stuff in very deeply when it is relayed in such a non-impactful way.

I hope to make enough of an impression on you here that you take in just how important having good awareness skills are. Not only that, but you become motivated to take action and actively practice being aware in your daily life.

Just by being more aware in your daily life, by stepping it up even a little bit, you will get a lot more out of the experience of life. That in itself should motivate you to be that bit more aware every day.

Our main focus here though, is awareness as it pertains to self defence, and there are three different levels to that: *situational awareness, self-awareness* and *threat awareness* (or threat recognition). Let's look at self-awareness first of all.

Self-Awareness

Unless you make a habit of getting into fights with dogs or grizzly bears or cute hamsters in pet shops that bite your finger when you try to pick them up (bastards!), then you would likely agree that when we practice self defence, we practice it with people in mind. That means we deal with other people and their behaviour every day. It would seem to make sense then that the more you know about people and how they act and why they do certain things, the better your interactions with others are going to be.

The more you know and understand about yourself, the better you will be able to understand about other people and their behaviour, because you can empathize with them and also quite often predict their behaviour.

It's therefore in your interests to be more self-aware and to try and understand why you are the way you are and why you do the things you do all the time. The more self-aware you are, the better you will be able to deal with people, even when they are being aggressive and violent.

"A human being has so many skins inside, covering the depths of the heart. We know so many things, but we don't know ourselves! Why, thirty or forty skins or hides, as thick and hard as an ox's or bear's, cover the soul. Go into your own ground and learn to know yourself there." **Eckhart Tolle**

A good level of self-awareness will allow you to be conscious of your strengths so that you can play to them better, and this includes in conflict situations. You will also know your weaknesses, which again will help you because you will know what about you needs developing.

Being self-aware will also reduce the chances of you behaving like an insensitive asshole and winding people up all the time. People who do this are quite often barely even aware that they are doing it. They just crash through life, oblivious most if the time of the damage they are doing.

A high level of self-awareness leads to good self-control and self-monitoring. You will think before you act (most of the time). These are all good things for helping you to avoid or defuse conflicts before they get physical.

Studies have also shown that those with good levels of self-awareness are more capable of handling their feelings and emotions, especially in times of stress. This is a good thing, especially considering just how highly stressful conflict and physical altercations can be. In such pressurised circumstances, the more self-control you can exert the better.

Discovery of the self is an on-going, continuous process which, at times, can be painful as hidden aspects are slowly uncovered. When confronted with difficult situations such as violent conflicts, we are expected to behave in a certain way, although feelings of vulnerability and uncertainty may challenge our perceived abilities. Being more self-aware can help us to cope in such circumstances, helping us to respect our fears, anxieties and concerns, and prompting questions about how these could be overcome.

Self-awareness is quite a deep subject as you can see. It also has many applications for self defence. Get to work on it.

Exercise

Reflect on a time when you found yourself in conflict with someone, or a time when you had to physically fight someone, a time when your feelings may have influenced your thoughts and behaviour. Did you feel in control of the situation? Did your emotions affect your level of confidence in this situation or how you perceived others?

Emotions can prompt action and inaction, intervention and withdrawal. Write your thoughts down or discuss this occasion with a friend.

Situational Awareness

Situational awareness is all about being tuned in to your surrounding environment. It's about being aware of what's going around you.

We lead such stressful and busy lives these days that it is easy to walk around in a very "switched off" state, where all of our attention is directed towards what is going on inside our head (or on the screen of our iphones!), rather than to what is going on around us.

When you're switched off it can be hard to detect changes in your environment or notice things that are out of place or not quite right. You could be walking into danger and you wouldn't even know it until it was too late.

To maintain situational awareness you must be switched on at all times. To be switched on is not to be in a state of hyper vigilance that borders on paranoia and makes you suspicious of everything. Instead, to be switched on is to be in a state of ***relaxed alertness***, which means you go about your daily business as usual but you maintain your awareness always.

This is mostly an unconscious process that runs in the background of your mind, meaning you can go about your business while still maintaining a good level of awareness.

Obviously, if you find yourself in unfamiliar environments, or environments that are known to be trouble spots, then you would up your awareness levels, but again, not to the point where you become wound up tight and jump at the slightest noise or movement. You are still relaxed, but your senses are on high alert.

Maintaining a switched on state in your daily life will help you avoid trouble, because a lot of the time, you will notice trouble well before it is on top of you and it is too late to do anything about it. You will spot potentially troublesome people and groups of people in time to either avoid them or keep a close eye on them. You will notice dodgy looking areas up ahead so you can take a different route and avoid them. And if trouble does come suddenly and unexpectedly (as it sometimes does) you should be ready to react in a way that will at least give you a chance.

Practice Drill

This is a good drill for enhancing your awareness and observation skills. As you go about your business you must spot people who are wearing a certain item of clothing. So for instance, you may elect to notice only those people who are wearing a red item of clothing or a blue item of clothing. It doesn't really matter which. The idea is just to focus your attention on one particular group of people. By doing this, you are forcing yourself to become aware of everyone around you as you filter out the ones who aren't in your chosen group. You can do this drill while you wait outside a shop on your partner (as I often do!) or while you are sitting on a bus or wherever. Just be casual about it. You'll be surprised how much you end up observing just by doing this drill.

Threat Awareness

Threat awareness, or threat recognition, is having the ability to spot a threat to your person before it does you any kind of harm.

This can mean seeing a particular kind of threat from a distance, such as a gang hanging on a street corner, or picking up on threatening behaviour from someone who is in your immediate vicinity.

If you are switched on enough you should be able to spot distant threats and avoid them. Another example of this would be if you are in a bar and someone was staring at you in a threatening manner from across the way. You would know to avoid that person then, or to keep a close eye on them, rather than not notice them at all and perhaps be blindsided by them later.

Awareness also comes into the equation when an aggressor is right in front of you. You need to be able to spot the signs that your aggressor is going to go from aggressive to violent. These signs are called pre-contact cues and include the following:

- "Grooming" -- fiddling with hair, face, ears, eyes, hat, etc, basically hands on the head/face area rubbing or smoothing, etc.
- The 3-6-9 glance, checking from side to side just before they attack
- The planted step, or setting their base just before they hit you
- Clenching of the teeth and setting of the jaw
- Verbal descends into monosyllables—"Yeah", "And", "So", "What"
- Closing of distance

Those are just some of the pre-contact cues to watch out for when facing off against an aggressor. Spot them early and you will have a better chance of acting before they do.

"Your new attitude should include an awareness of where you are and what's going on around you. It's like when you're driving: you check the rearview mirror, watch for flashing brake lights up ahead, quickly rehearse the turns you'll be making... all at once." **Stanford Strong**

4 LEARN TO COMMUNICATE

"The single biggest problem in communication is the illusion that it has taken place." **George Bernard Shaw**

When it comes to how we communicate with each other (especially in a self defence situation), the words we choose in our exchanges are less important than how we actually put those words across. Being an enlightened and educated reader, I'm sure you know this already.

I'm also sure that you are aware of the following:

Only a small percentage of communication involves actual words: 7%, to be exact. In fact, 55% of communication is visual (body language, eye contact) and 38% is vocal (pitch, speed, volume, tone of voice).

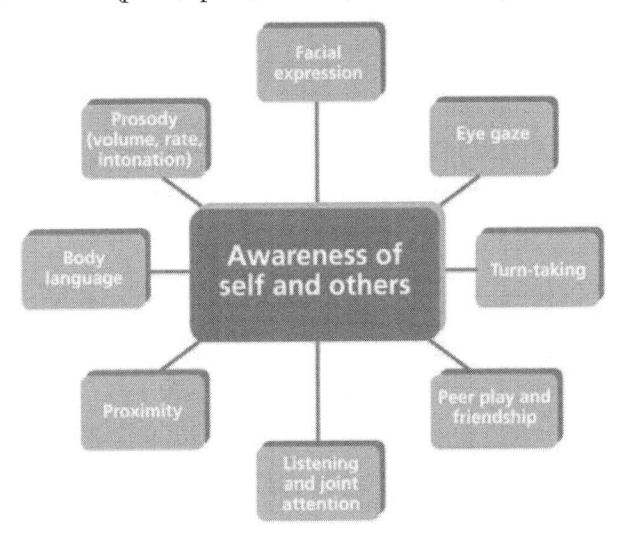

Given these statistics, when it comes to dealing with a potential threat or threats in conflict situation, we can see that it is our body language that will have the biggest bearing on whether or not the outcome of said situation will be in our favour.

Or to put it in simpler terms: How you present yourself to a potential threat will decide whether that threat sees you as predator or prey.

The Four Levels Of Communication

Broadly speaking, there are four levels of communication in self defence:

1. Non-Fight Communication
2. Pre-Fight Communication
3. In-Fight Communication
4. Post-Fight Communication

Let's look at each of these in turn.

Non-Fight Communication

Non-fight communication is basically how you put yourself across in your daily life, those times when you are not involved in any kind of violent conflict (which is almost all the time for most of us).

Thugs, street hustlers, predators, when they look for a victim, one of the first things they look for in a person is how they carry themselves.

Think about it. If you're a predator looking for prey, who do you go for? The person who carries themselves with confidence and moves with assured purpose, or the person who carries themselves meekly, who acts unsure of themselves and who gives out victim vibes?

There are other factors involved in choosing a victim, of course, but body language is a clear indicator of victim suitability.

Making yourself a hard target for those who wish to harm or take advantage, starts with how you put yourself across to the world around you.

What kind of person do you want to be? What kind of person do you need to be in order to make yourself a harder target for criminals?

This is fundamental. If you don't have confidence in yourself, if you are unsure of yourself, if you are meek in front of others, people will notice, because your body language (as well as your words and tone of voice) will communicate this.

In the case of criminals, they will hone in on the kind of vibe you are putting out. They don't see a person with issues, they see an easy target.

Street criminals want minimum fuss from their victims. They just want to do what they have to do and move safely on to the next victim. They try not to choose people who look like they would put up too much of a fuss, who will probably fight back and not take too kindly to being hassled in such a way.

You have to put out the same vibe; you have to communicate with your body language that you do not fit the normal victim profile.

Not fitting the victim profile will ensure you lead a relatively un-victimised life.

Despite our best efforts though, shit still happens sometimes. Some people just insist on trying it on anyway, and this is where the next level of communication comes in.

Pre-Fight Communication

The way in which you communicate in the early stages of a potentially violent conflict is vitally important.

If someone does decide to test you in a threatening manner, you still need to put yourself across with confidence and self-assurance. You have to look like you are not rattled by the situation, even though internally, you may well be.

When you fence a potential threat, you are not just controlling your personal space; you are communicating your intentions to the threat.

And your intentions are: to try to diffuse the situation non-violently, but if need be, you will use violence and do so without hesitation.

Put another way, you are drawing a line in the sand and letting it be known that the consequences of crossing that line will be severe.

The threat will pick up on this vibe, if only subconsciously. Many situations can be diffused straight away just by presenting yourself to the threat in front of you in such an assertive manner.

If the threat has misjudged you, that will become obvious to them in your demeanour and they will most likely retreat.

Sometimes, that's all it takes.

Other times, for whatever reason, violence becomes inevitable. Communication however, does not stop there.

In-Fight Communication

If you hit first and hit hard, you are sending a message, a very clear message to the person you just hit that they chose the wrong person. They'll get it when they wake up.

If you get into a fight, your every strike, your every movement, has to hammer home the same message:

YOU FUCKED WITH THE WRONG ONE!

Meaning you have to go in hard and fast to overwhelm the threat, to do the exact opposite of what they expected you to do.

You are not just attacking the body but the mind as well.

You're trying to break their will, beat down the bad intentions in them.

Put the fight out of them- literally and figuratively.

Even during the fight, you give verbal commands: "STAY DOWN! DON'T MOVE!"

If there are other threats around, this will communicate a message to them as well: Try anything and you'll get the same.

Post-Fight Communication

This is the final level of communication in self defence, the post-fight communication. The way in which you put yourself across here is most important, especially if you have to deal with the law and explain your actions in court.

All you have at this stage, no matter what happened previously, is your ability to communicate.

Many people fall foul of the law due to bad or ineffective communication skills. If you come across as arrogant or cocky to the police, or if you are unable to justify your actions in court, you will suffer the consequences, which could mean jail time.

If you don't want to get swallowed up whole by the judicial system you must know exactly what to say and exactly how you should put yourself across. You must learn good articulation skills, which means making the practice of such skills a part of your self defence training.

If you are unsure of how to communicate properly post-fight, then I suggest you read *Facing Violence*, by Rory Miller. In that book you will learn all about how to put yourself across to the law afterwards.

Learn To Communicate Effectively

Communication is fundamental in self defence.

Physical skills matter less than the ability to communicate effectively, and on all levels.

When you walk down the street, when you are faced by a potential threat, when you have to physically deal with a threat and when you have to explain your actions afterwards, you have to be vitally aware of what you are communicating at all times through your body language, your tone of voice and with your choice of words.

Self defence is not just about hitting someone.

Learning to communicate in the right way will save you a lot of trouble in the long run.

Practice Drill

Be conscious of how you present yourself in public. How are you coming across to other people? Do you carry yourself with confidence or are you unsure of yourself? For the next while, be aware of how you walk, how you stand and how you talk to people. Try to present yourself as being a confident and assertive type. I don't mean you have to be arrogant and in everybody's faces. You can be quietly confident as well. Just do what fits your personality, even if it feels like acting at first, eventually you will begin to feel more sure of yourself for real.

Another drill you can do is the Articulation Drill. Play out a self defence scenario and then afterwards, explain your actions like you are explaining them to the police after the incident. When you are finished a partner will play the role of the bad guy and put across his side of the story, or they will play the role of a cop and question your statement. The goal here is to work on your post-fight communication and practice justifying your actions in the eyes of the law.

5 KNOW YOURSELF

"One's own self is well hidden from one's own self; of all mines of treasure, one's own is the last to be dug up."
Friedrich Wilhelm Nietzsche

You must learn to control your own mind as much as possible if you want to have the bottle to fight when you need too.

Through working doors and training in Combatives, I have realised the importance of being in the right mindset when it comes to engaging in real violence.

But we hear that all the time, don't we, people talking about the right mindset? So how do we get that mindset?

Well first of all, I believe you have to square it with yourself that if you are left with no choice, that you absolutely will, without hesitation, go like fuck and put the other person down.

In the midst of a confrontation is not the time to be debating this. This will only cause indecision, which will lead to hesitation and most likely failure to act when you need too.

You must make a pact with yourself that you will act when you have to and also have the self-belief to carry that through. You must be steadfast in this decision.

At a certain point in a confrontation, when you believe that things are about to take a turn for the worse, you must have the ability to flick an internal switch that allows you to access cold aggression and a forward drive mentality, only hitting the off switch when the situation has been dealt with, which usually means your opponent lying on the ground and unable or unwilling to cause you any more aggro.

The fear of violence is very deep rooted and I'm not

advocating that you try and eradicate it because it can't be done. That fear is there for a reason. But when your life is on the line, you need the ability to act despite that fear.

There are many reasons why some people don't act when they need to, so you need to go deep and find out what issues are surrounding your inability to act when you need to.

For me, I had concerns about seriously injuring someone, which quite often meant I didn't take action when I needed too. But over time, I worked on this issue and told myself that if I didn't take action then I may just end up being the person who is seriously injured. Once I realised this, I felt better able to hit when I had to.

Such issues are not easy to get rid of. To this day I will always try to use low force options to sort out a situation. However, if I feel the situation calls for it, I am fully prepared to use more damaging options.

If you happen to struggle with finding that willingness to act, it could also be because you don't get angry enough. I have found anger to be very good for displacing fear. You must say to yourself, *"Who does this person think they are, bullying me like this? What right do they have to treat me in this way?* WHO THE FUCK DOES THIS CUNT THINK HE IS? WELL FUCK HIM, I'M NOT STANDING FOR THIS SHIT!"

You get the idea? You're riling yourself up for action through the use of self-righteous anger and moral indignation. When you are angry, you are not afraid so you will find it much easier to go for it then.

So strengthening your bottle for real violence, finding that will to act, is about doing proper Combatives training that addresses all stages of a violent confrontation and doing so in a realistic way that makes you tougher, mentally and physically, and allows you to practice accessing a good combative mindset that will make it possible for you to act when you have to.

It is also about doing internal work, discovering what

issues you have around the use of violence (morally and ethically) and also what kind of person you are. If you are too timid, what steps can you take to become more assertive? How can you practice being assertive? Do you value yourself enough to not let people push you around? If not, why not? These are the questions you must ask yourself.

Your Capacity For (Survival) Violence

Could you gouge someone's eye out if you had too?

There is a big difference between saying you could do something and actually doing it.

You may be fully capable of gouging out someone's eye, but you may not have the capacity to do so when needed to.

The truth be told, I don't know if I could gouge someone's eye completely out of its socket so that it is hanging there like some gruesome conker.

I'd like to think I could relieve someone of their sight in such a horrific way, if I really had to do so.

If someone where trying to kill me, for instance, I'd like to think I would dislodge that blob of jelly in a heartbeat if it meant I was going to stay alive a bit longer.

The truth is however, I will never really know until I am put in that situation.

I may freeze.

I don't know.

And that's one of the paradoxes about self defence training: *You will never really know if any of what you are training will work until you actually have to use the stuff for real.*

We can be *almost* sure of our training, yeah, based on other factors, like physics, combative principles, past experiences, the experiences of other people who have been there, but…

You yourself will never know for sure.

And there is nothing you can do about that except go out and test the stuff for real. That's a road I have been down. I got into bouncing, but obviously that isn't for everyone, so in a moment we will look at a different way to get that experience.

In the meantime, how can we narrow the gap between what we are capable of, and what we have the capacity to actually do (gaining experience aside, that is)?

Capability And Capacity (Or All Talk And No Action)

Before we answer that question though, let's look at the two concepts of capability and capacity in a bit more detail.

As Rory Miller puts it in *Facing Violence: Preparing for the Unexpected* , capability is a psychical skill. You do Combatives or martial arts, you can therefore hurt someone.

Not everyone is emotionally equipped to hurt another human being however. If the thought of doing so makes you uneasy, then it's safe to say you have a low capacity for inflicting violence.

And maybe no capacity for survival-violence—the kill or be killed type of violence that is intended to inflict maximum damage on the other person.

That can be fixed however—to an extent. The fact that you are aware of your capacity levels, and the fact that you are acknowledging them, is enough to increase those levels somewhat.

After that you have to scrutinise your capacity levels and decide if they are really true or not. You may automatically think you don't have the capacity for doing a certain thing—ripping of an ear, for instance—but on closer examination you find that the idea is not that repulsive to you, at least not enough to put you off from doing it if you really had to.

When put in a situation where you have to fight for your life, your capacity for survival-violence will increase. Your in-built survival mechanism will insist on it.

Most people have the capacity for brutal violence. You

may think you don't, that your capacity for such things are non-existent, but believe me, it is there, buried deep within you, lying dormant and ready to be tapped under the right circumstances, or when stimulated in some way.

If this were not true, then we wouldn't have all those examples from history, where ordinary people have somehow found it in themselves to do horrible things to their fellow human beings, horrible things that include torture and cold-blooded murder. I live in a country where people maimed and killed each other for thirty years or more.

Human beings are capable of anything under the right circumstances.

You just have to look at your capacity for survival-violence and shed the light of reality on it—ask yourself, would I really be able to do these horrible things if my life (or the life of someone I loved) was on the line and I really had too?

For most people, the answer to that question would be a definite YES!

Some acts (of violence) can still be hard to imagine yourself doing however. Pay special attention to those acts because you are going to use them in the practice drill.

Before we proceed any further though, let's talk about something else that may prevent you from defending yourself to the fullest extent—social conditioning.

Social Conditioning

According to Wikipedia, social conditioning can be defined thus: "Social conditioning refers to the sociological process of training individuals in a society to respond in a manner generally approved by the society in general and peer groups within society. The concept ... [can also] determine their social actions and responses."

Social conditioning can have a profoundly powerful effect on a person, which is why it is utilised so much in our society. Good for maintaining the status quo, bad in many other ways, as we are about to find out.

You see, from a very early age we are taught to behave and react to things in a certain way. In the case of violence we are taught that it is wrong to hit another person and that there will be potentially severe consequences if we do.

This attitude is completely ingrained in us by the time we hit adulthood and it influences how we react to violence a great deal.

So when we need to use violence, even in self defence, our social conditioning reminds us of how wrong it is to hit a fellow human being and that the consequences for doing so could be grave.

(Interestingly, most criminals who seem to have no problem dishing out violence do so because they have a different social conditioning that makes it easy for them to "other" their victims so they can treat them like a resource or piece of meat instead of a real person, which makes it easier for them to do what they do. You want to be able inflict violence at the drop of a hat? Model the criminal mind.)

So no matter how good your training has been or how much faith you have in it, social conditioning can still kill your willingness to act, or at the very least, cause fatal indecision, and indecision is the last thing you want in a violent confrontation when a positive outcome depends wholly on being decisive and quick acting.

This is something I struggled with for a long time. I knew I had the physical skills to handle most of the situations I found myself in, but somewhere in my mind, something was causing me to hesitate or even not strike out at all.

This is very serious because it can cause great anxiety and further feelings of fear. It can also completely kill your confidence in such situations because you will inevitably beat yourself up (after your attacker has, of course) over the fact that you didn't act when you should have.

In short, you will feel like a failure and the next time

you find yourself up against someone, your past experiences of perceived failure will come flooding back, along with a load more fear. It becomes like a vicious cycle.

Even when I was bouncing, this social conditioning was constantly reinforced by the management of the places in which I worked. It was made clear that hitting the punters was frowned upon and could end up in a loss of your job. Even if the punter attacked you first! You were forced into doing your job with one hand tied behind your back.

It is because of this very powerful social conditioning that many people are unable to act when they should in a violent confrontation, because some Nanny-like figure is in the back of their mind waving their finger at them to signal no, don't do it or else.

Well, I learned that you have to take that finger-waving bitch and shoot her in the head!

You are a grown up, a very intelligent person who is fully capable of making justifiable force decisions. You do not need the equivalent of the Nanny State inside your head telling you what to do when your life is potentially on the line.

Like most things, it comes down to just being aware that these hindrances to performance exist and after that acknowledging their presence before kindly telling them to fuck off out of it.

For me that was enough. The social conditioning was no longer subconscious and I could consciously over-ride it. I also worked on changing my beliefs about violence, challenging what I was taught about it.

I made sure I knew when it was justified—ethically, morally and lawfully— to hit someone. I developed certain boundaries that if crossed by someone else would result in a violent response from me.

I did all this head-work when I was bouncing so I was able to change myself very quickly, only because I was given many chances to do so through the job, many chances to put myself to the test and consciously over-ride the social conditioning we've been discussing here.

Survival-Violence Capacity Exercise

Before we begin with this, I should warn you that this exercise is pretty dark and it will take you to some horrible, disgusting places. It is necessary to go to these places however, if you want to increase your capacity for survival-violence (read, brutal violence).

And as awful as that sounds, we should remember that the kind of violence we are talking about here will only be used in life or death situations. We are not talking about social violence here, like a fight outside the chippy on a Saturday night. We are talking instead of asocial violence, predator violence; the kind of violence that may severely injure you or take your life.

Brutal violence must unfortunately be met with equally brutal violence–survival-violence. You are kidding yourself if you think it can be dealt with by anything less.

So let's proceed. Get yourself nice and comfortable, preferably doing a relaxation exercise first.

Once you are nice and relaxed, start to think of a situation where you would have to fight for your life. It could be a mugging gotten out of hand or some psycho trying to stab you to death for the pleasure of it, or even a rape scenario. Try to make the scenario as plausible as possible, like a situation you could actually find yourself in if you were having a really bad day and luck had abandoned you.

Okay, put yourself in the scene, engage as many of your senses as possible, at least three of them. Now put yourself into the fight. Put yourself in a position where you have to do something horrible to your attacker in order to save yourself—preferably one of the violent acts that you struggled with imagining yourself doing earlier, one that really turns your stomach, like gouging out both his eyes, or ripping of his ear, or biting of his nose.

Vividly imagine how that would feel— the texture of his flesh, the coppery taste of his blood, the warmth of it spilling into your mouth. Yes it's disgusting. But your life is on the line here. If you don't act you will get killed. This is survival. You have to do what you have to do.

Feel the powerful force of righteous indignation coursing through you. Use it to fuel your actions.

See yourself causing damage to your attacker until you are able to completely stop the attack.

See yourself handling the situation.

Tell yourself that you can do anything you have to do to survive, without a second thought, you just do it.

You survive.

You're a survivor.

Believe that.

Okay, now, wipe the slate clean in your mind. Take yourself out of the previous scenario.

Now I want you to imagine a different scenario in which you will solve the situation without having to use violence. You will see yourself escaping or avoiding the threat altogether, or you will defuse the situation through dialogue.

This is important. Make sure you do this.

For every scenario you create in which you have to use violence, create another scenario where you don't use violence.

Vividly imagining violent scenes like the one above will have a negative impact on your psyche over time. It will alter your character and you will possibly end up in a lot of violent situations in real life.

The mind cannot really distinguish between fantasy and reality. You most likely know this already. Creating such vivid scenes can actually attract more of the same into your life (it works both ways: positive stuff can be attracted also).

So we balance the negative with the positive. Hence the

non-violent scenario.

Repeated practice of this exercise will help to burn new neural pathways into your brain, just as if you actually did the things you imagined for real.

It's very powerful stuff, which is why you have to be so careful about balancing the positive and the negative.

This is the only way to increase your capacity for survival-violence without actually being brutally violent in reality.

6 LEARN TO MANAGE FEAR AND ADRENALINE

"There are times when fear is good. It must keep its watchful place at the heart's controls." **Aeschylus**

This is by far the longest chapter in this book, and that's because fear and adrenaline play a massive part in the self defence equation, so I thought it worth it to spend a bit of time on the subjects. So let's get going.

Handled incorrectly, fear and adrenaline can really do a number on a person, turning them from normal to quivering wreck in a heartbeat.

The best plans, the best intentions, can be decimated in the wake of these two titans of mind-body control.

Despite the havoc they wreak on a person, these individual reactions are completely benign. They hold no more malevolence than a hurricane which passes through a town and leaves the town in splinters and its inhabitants desolate and traumatised, even dead.

You can't apply human constructs of morality against what is only natural in the world. A hurricane is a hurricane. It is what it is.

Likewise, fear is fear; adrenaline is adrenaline. Natural occurrences in a natural system.

The Human Bio-Computer
Or to put it another way, essential software in a finely programmed bio-computer.

They exist to help.

It's your fault if you can't control them properly. You can't blame the response. You must find the correct process to follow so you can control those responses.

That's on you as well.

You are the end user of the bio-computer in question. It is up to you to program that computer so that it runs right and does exactly what you want it to do.

If a program is not running the way you want it too then you must re-configure it until it does.

The hard part is figuring out just how to reconfigure the programme.

If your own fear and adrenal responses are currently crippling your ability to act in a violent confrontation, it is because you have not developed a suitable control mechanism for them both.

Kinda like a temperature gauge that you can turn down if it starts to get too hot.

Or an over-ride switch that you can hit whenever you need too, something that allows you to act despite what you are feeling in your mind and body.

Unfortunately, we have yet to get to the stage where re-programming ourselves is as easy as re-programming a real computer.

So I suggest to you here that changing our behaviour and our reactions to things is more of an art than a science. That's what I've found anyway. It's an on-going process. There is no magical switch to hit unfortunately.

In computer programming terms it's the equivalent of sitting down and coding and re-coding an entirely new program, and then perhaps doing the same with many of the other programs that relate to it. After that it's a never-ending process of checking and tweaking to make sure the programs are still running correctly, and also to make continual improvements, for we can always be better, can't we?

In the case of fear, and of adrenaline, we have to constantly work on managing our reactions to them. To do that we must turn our full attention on them and we must come to know them intimately.

You must totally familiarise yourself with every aspect

of them, which means not running away from them, which can be hard in the case of fear and adrenaline. They are bogey-men, after all.

They are also inextricably linked. Both are part of our survival mechanism. That should give you a clue as to their importance. They help keep us alive in dangerous situations. We need fear and we need adrenaline, especially in extreme stress situations like in a violent confrontation with someone who is trying to kill us.

The key to handling both fear and adrenaline is realising and accepting that they will always be present in high-stress situations like violent confrontations.

I could end this chapter right here. That one sentence contains everything you need to know about learning to handle your own fear and adrenal response. You just have to let the truth of it sink in.

The fear response and the adrenal response are very much different sides of the same coin. One almost always accompanies the other. However, it may help us if we consider them separate for a moment and look at each response in turn.

Fight Adrenaline

It really helps to know the physiological response to adrenaline, since like I've already said, you need to know a thing intimately in order to become truly comfortable with it, and also in order to control it.

For this book I am more interested in the psychology attached to adrenal response management, and the type of training we need to do in order to manage it effectively.

One of the main reasons why so many people handle adrenal dump so badly is because it is a completely alien (and thus terrifying) feeling to them.

Back in the day when we used to live like the Flintstones, danger in the form of huge beasts was always right around the corner. The adrenal response came in pretty handy back then when you had to try and outrun a ten ton hairy beast with massive teeth that would cut you in half with one bite.

Living in that kind of environment you soon got used to feeling adrenal dump. It was a completely natural feeling and one that was probably welcomed if it helped get you out of danger.

These days, hairy beasts with big teeth can usually only be found at amateur porn sites. They may be scary but I doubt they would bring on adrenal dump, unless one of them tried to sit on you…

My point (yes, there is a point!) is that we live pretty safe and secure life's now, despite what the news would have you believe. It's perfectly possible for some people to go a whole lifetime without ever experiencing the adrenal dump brought on by a violent confrontation.

Most people will experience it at some time or other, however, and when they do, their internal wiring tends to go a bit awry. Things stop working the way they are supposed to. *What's happening to me?* they cry inside. *Why do I feel like this? Am I dying? Oh God, oh Jesus…I'm fucking terrified!*

It can feel quite bad. Sickening.

Still, the more you experience it, the more comfortable you become with it, if comfortable is the right word. Maybe functional is a better word. Not quite so incapacitated.

Exposure therapy (incorporating proper training) and education. These two things will help you remain functional under the influence of fight adrenaline.

Study its effects. Get to know the biology of it, the psychology of it. Learn to view it as a completely normal and helpful response. Or like a superpower, whichever one floats your boat.

In any case, don't dread its onset. Learn to welcome it instead.

The enemy is in front of you. Not within you.

Adrenal Stress Training

Training will certainly help a great deal. Okay, so your experience of adrenaline in the gym will never match the real thing, but training still helps.

Train with real intensity. Bring your imagination into it. Keep it as close to the bone as possible without getting seriously injured.

Find a good instructor who can take you a little beyond your limits each time without actually breaking you. Your confidence will grow and you will become better equipped to handle the adrenal response in a real violent confrontation.

Put yourself in other situations where you may feel adrenaline. Do some public speaking. That never fails to bring on the adrenal response in me.

Learn to be present with the response. Don't try to pretend it isn't there. That doesn't work and will cause anxiety and even fear.

Instead, acknowledge that the adrenaline is there, acknowledge how it is making you feel and just sit in it.

Float in it. Just try to float in it and stay calm. Then do what you gotta do.

It will always be unpleasant. But I guess if it was pleasant we wouldn't feel as compelled to do something with it, like try to get rid of it through focused action (or fighting back).

Adrenaline is what it is. You can't change it. It is a perfect human response to danger. Completely pure.

And it works like a charm every single time.

Your reaction to it may leave a lot to be desired, but that reaction can be changed, through proper training—mental and physical conditioning, intellectual and dare I say it, philosophical study.

Managing fight adrenaline is only really a problem in the pre-fight phase of a confrontation. Once things kick off it's not really something to worry too much about. But as I've said before, handling the pre-fight phase correctly is essential to a positive outcome, so therefore handling fight adrenaline is essential to a positive outcome as well.

Changing your reaction to adrenal stress comes down to motivation: how much do you want to learn to perform well under adrenal stress conditions?

If you are motivated enough you will go to surprising lengths to achieve that end. I went as far as spending my weekends working as a bouncer in pubs and clubs for years, exposing myself to situations that brought on the kind of adrenal response we've been talking about here.

Did that help me? Yes, of course it did.

Am I completely comfortable with the feelings of adrenaline now? No, not at all. It still turns me sick and I hate how physically draining it can be.

But I have learned to perform reasonably well under the influence of adrenaline, because I was motivated to do so.

You may not choose to go as far as becoming a doorman. You may instead choose to pit yourself against a padded assailant on a regular basis, or indulge in full contact sparring. Whatever. It's all good training. Whatever you do, it's better than nothing.

Fear

Just like adrenaline, fear has to be managed or it will turn you into a useless quivering wreck.

I'm speaking from experience here.

I remember one of the first big incidents I had to face in my early days on the door. It was myself and two other doormen against six big farmer types who didn't take too kindly to their mate being turfed out on his ear earlier in the night. Arguments ensued and things quickly escalated. Plate glass windows were kicked in and shards of glass covered the whole floor of the foyer.

I was about twenty years of age at that time. I hadn't seen much action up till then and the fear I was feeling gripped me like a vice. The accompanying adrenaline drained every bit of colour out of my face.

I just remember being in the midst of this totally chaotic situation and feeling oddly disconnected from the whole thing, like I was an observer in some parallel universe. I was too scared to even move at one point. It took one of the other doormen being ganged up on to force me into action again.

Things finally got sorted out after what seemed like an age. The manager came and ushered me and the other two doormen out the back door, since the guys we were fighting wouldn't calm down while we were there. The police were called and we left the rest to them.

I have never felt fear like I did then, before or since. It was an intense experience, not to mention a valuable lesson in how crippling fear can be if you let it.

What I learned that night was that you had to stay active, you had to keep facing the music, so to speak. Backing away only worsened the feelings of fear and made it harder to get going again.

Real Fear And Psychological Fear

Before we go any further we have to make a distinction between real fear and psychological fear.

Real fear is what you feel when you are in imminent danger. It's a part of your survival mechanism and as such is there to help you.

It is what you feel in most violent confrontations, for obvious reasons. Being in a violent confrontation means that you are in harm's way. Your brain will therefore send the fear signal to kick-start your adrenaline so you can run or fight.

Just like with the adrenal response, the fear response is completely natural and there isn't much you can do to get rid of it. It's there and that's all there is to it. You just have to deal with it.

Psychological fear is ego based and has nothing to do with your survival mechanism. It is all in your mind.

To use a familiar acronym, this type of fear is False Evidence Appearing Real.

When you feel psychological fear it is because your ego feels under threat. There is no real danger present, nothing there that would physically harm you in any way.

The danger, if you can call it that, is in the form of perceived humiliation, failure, wondering what others will say about you, or because you are stepping outside of your comfort zone.

This is a different type of fear and one that I won't be addressing in this article. In this article I want to look at real fear, the fear that comes from when someone is about to attack you.

You'll notice I said when someone is about to attack you. When you have been attacked and you are in fight mode, in my experience fear isn't usually a problem because you are so focused on surviving the encounter.

Fear is essentially a warning signal that danger is imminent. So when you are facing an aggressor intent on violence those warning signals will be firing of like crazy in order to get you to take some kind of action that will neutralise the danger. Hence fight or flight.

When you are in fight mode however, you don't have time to feel fear because you are so focused on the fight. In actuality, you tend to feel more calmness than fear. A tiny voice in the back of your mind may even be saying, Hey, this isn't so bad actually, I'm dealing with this and this guy I'm fighting, he isn't really up to much. What was I so afraid off anyway?

Once again it is the pre-fight stage that is the problem, the build-up of tension and fear before-hand. If you let fear get a grip on you at this stage, you won't take proactive action and instead you will be at the mercy of your aggressor.

Methods For Managing Fear
So what methods can we use to help manage our fear?

We can't eliminate it, no more than adrenaline. It will always be there to some degree or another, depending on how much experience you have in dealing with violent confrontations.

As a doorman I ended up in quite a lot of violent confrontations. It was my job to sort them out, after all. Repeated exposure to such situations definitely helped to lessen the fear I was feeling, but it didn't eliminate it.

(Only sociopaths don't feel fear like the rest of us and unless your name is Patrick Bateman, it's doubtful you're a sociopath, and if you are, don't you have your next victim to stalk? Just saying.)

The way to tackle fear in a violent confrontation is to first mould yourself into someone who is able to handle it.

That's why we train, is it not? To reinforce our minds and bodies so they can withstand the effects of high stress.

So that's where we will start, with the training.

Combatives Training

Combatives training is the only kind of training that really counts when it comes to hammering the mind and body into shape in preparation for a violent confrontation.

Martial arts training takes way too long and still doesn't cut it in the end. Combat sports training, although probably better than martial arts training in terms of physical and mental conditioning, doesn't quite cut it either. The goals are different. The training methods are different.

Combatives' trains people to handle real violence from the start. There are no rules involved, no rituals to follow, no belt ladder to climb or trophies to hold high; no fluff of any kind. Combatives is all about what works in a fight.

It stands to reason then, that if you do this type of training on a regular basis, you will be much more confident about your chances should you end up involved in a violent confrontation.

Combatives training quite literally exploded my self-confidence. I also see it explode the confidence of my students and private clients, far more so than any martial arts student I've had in the past.

And this is because you are training to handle real violence, not fantasy violence. The stuff you learn in Combatives is as practical as it gets. And because it is all pressure tested on a regular basis you get to experience just how well it all works (within reason).

What I am getting at here is that you need to have faith in your training. Some of you reading this may have religious faith, faith that God will keep you safe in your life. Well, having faith in your training is the same thing.

You must choose to believe that your training will get you through whatever situation you find yourself in, be it against one attacker or many.

I have great faith in my training. When I was working doors I took a lot of strength from that faith. And guess what?

It helped me deal with whatever fear I was feeling. I knew–I knew– my training would carry me through and it always did. Not once did it let me down when I needed it.

You have all that power behind you; the power of faith, the power of your training and the whole arsenal of tools and tactics you have gleaned from it.

YOU CAN'T LOOSE!

How could you?

There is only one thing that may let you down in the end and that is social conditioning, which we have already discussed.

Supra States

A supra state is the wilful creation of a split in the personality to create a persona that can deal effectively with violent confrontation. The conspiracy theorists among you will recognise this principle technique as being the foundation for MK-ULTRA, the CIA mind control experiment started in the 1970's.

Supra states in the context we are talking about are not quite so sinister however. It basically involves you creating another persona for yourself, one which you will only go into when you have to really put someone down.

To quote Lee Morrison:

"This is like a shotgun under an overcoat that would only be called upon worst case scenario, outside of that it remains tightly covert and boxed away. The control of such a mindset will allow anyone to control their emotions during the full spectrum of a violent event."

If you think about it we all take on different personas when we are with different people and in different situations. What we are talking about here is the same thing, just having a separate persona in place for when we have to dish out violence.

The value of this technique is obvious. By assuming the guise of this one-dimensional persona (whose sole purpose is to inflict violence) we can bypass all the usual baggage and hang-ups we have normally, all the social conditioning we have been talking about.

If you are good at imagining and visualisation then you should have little problem in creating this persona and installing it into your mind. You can then use an anchor to call upon this persona in times of need.

Tactical Arousal Control Techniques

Tactical Arousal Control Techniques (or TACT for short) are techniques that are used to keep you calm and focused in high stress situations.

The most common form of TACT is Tactical Breathing. There are few different variations on this, including combat breathing, four-count breathing and diaphragmatic breathing. Choose whichever one works best for you.

We also have what are called Centering Techniques, which derive from traditional martial arts. Centering involves taking a deep breath and on exhalation allowing all of your awareness to settle in your centre of gravity, bringing about a sensation of inner calm. I've found this particular technique to be quite useful when under stress.

A more advanced form of centering involves the use of an image as you breathe out. On exhalation picture something light like a feather or a leaf, slowly, slowly drifting down in front of you, until it stops and hovers just at the height of your belly button. The purpose of the image is to enhance the relaxation effects of the breath. Try it, it works really well.

Practice the exercise with your eyes closed at first. Then when you get comfortable with it, do it with your eyes open. The goal is to be able to do it with eyes open while still maintaining situational awareness, which isn't as hard as you think. It just takes practice.

And just so you are not floating in some far away over-relaxed state after using this technique, you can add on a "command action", a one-word command to bring you into sharp focus and attention. Once you are in the relaxed state, say to yourself something like "focus" or even "scan" to bring yourself fully into the present situation will still maintaining your sense of inner calm and relaxation.

Muscle relaxation techniques are another option, but these must be practiced quite a bit before trying to use them in an actual situation. You must first make that mind-body connection, making it stronger with every practice. In the beginning it will take about fifteen minutes or so for you to get rid of muscular tension and get really relaxed. After a fair bit of practice you should be able to bring about this state instantly.

7 LEARN SITUATIONAL CONTROL SKILLS

"No situational control = you're going down." **Neal Martin**

I don't care how good your punch is, or how many techniques you happen to know. The bottom line is that if you can't control the pre-fight you don't stand a chance of winning the fight overall.

I know this from bitter experience. Let me tell you a story from my early bouncing days.

I was on the door one night and I'd only been doing the job a couple of months. I was green. I knew jack shit about proper violence, except what I'd learned through martial arts training, which wasn't much.

I was ignorant to the concepts of situational control and pre-emptive striking and I was about to suffer the consequences of that ignorance.

So I was alone at the front door of the shit-hole pub I was working in and one of the regulars, who had been tossed out earlier in the night, approaches me and demands to speak to the head doorman. I politely told him he would have to wait to later on, that the head doorman was upstairs in the club and otherwise engaged.

The guy was persistent. He demanded to be let in. At this point he was right inside in my personal space. A few of his mates had also gathered outside as well. He continued to ask to be let in and was getting steadily more agitated.

I kept my cool, but I was allowing him to control the situation. I should have been more assertive and either told him to clear off or just shut the door in his face.

Violence was impending but I was too naive to see it

coming.

I saw him look left, then right (a classic pre-contact cue) and then I felt his fist smash into my forehead and I reeled back into the hallway, instinctively grabbing on to the guy as I did so.

I ended up on the floor with him on top of me. For a few seconds I couldn't think what to do. Luckily neither could he. He threw a punch at my face which I managed to slap aside.

Years of martial arts training wasn't really helping me much here. I eventually slapped my hands over both his ears, but not hard enough to really impact him much.

At this point he got to his feet and grabbed my leg, and then he began to pull me across the floor. His mates stood outside in the street like a pack of hungry wolves, egging him on. They wanted me outside so they could go to work on me properly. I felt helpless.

Luckily, one of the other doormen came running down the stairs at this point and got the guy off me. I jumped to my feet, shaken, but otherwise fine. A few punches were thrown by me and the other doorman as we forced the guy outside to the street so we could finally close the door on him and his mates.

So that was a harsh lesson. I never let anyone get that close to me again.

Defining Situational Control

Situational control is the art of controlling the pre-fight stage of a violent confrontation. How you handle the pre-fight will determine the outcome of the fight over all, whether you win or lose.

Mismanage the pre-fight and the consequences can be very serious, which is why it is so important to learn situational control tactics.

In its most basic form, situational control means just as it sounds: you maintain control of the situation from start to finish as best you can so as to affect a favourable outcome. The pre-fight stage is where you will be able to affect the most control. If it goes to fight stage it becomes difficult to exert any control except through the use of violence, but things tend to be very spontaneous and also very frantic, so maintaining control in that situation can be difficult. What happens happens.

Assert Yourself

As people go, I'm a pretty laid back sort of guy. My Dad always says that if I was any more laid back I'd be horizontal!

There is nothing wrong with being chilled and laid back. Being of that nature means I am a very tolerant and reasonable kind of guy. I don't fly of the handle easily with people, which means I am better able to listen to them and hopefully find a non-violent solution to whatever conflict is happening.

My laid back and diplomatic nature allows me to exhaust all possibilities before I even think about using violence on someone, which is after all, good practice as far as self protection goes. Violence should always be your last resort.

Don't feel bad if you are not the fighting type (an asshole in other wards). Sometimes your ego will chide you for allowing people to say certain things to you, and it will make you feel bad for not just lashing out in defence.

People may say bad things, even very hurtful things, but they are just words. To your ego it is fighting talk, but your ego doesn't know what it is talking about so don't feel bad for letting things go over your head. That's just good tactics that will save you from being involved in a violent incident.

Having said that, you need to know where to draw the line and you also have to be prepared to reprimand that person if they cross that line. If that means violence, then so be it. As the saying goes: *"Violence is not the answer, but when it is, it's the only answer"*.

Only you will know where that line is. Only you will know how much you can take. How long are you going to allow this person to try and bully you into submission or build up to hitting you?

I will always give people a chance. I will allow them to talk and shout all day if they want to, but if they cross the line into physical bullying by putting their hands on me or trying to encroach upon my personal space, then I will immediately assert myself in some way and make it clear that their advances are not welcome. If they continue to push things then I will be left with no choice but to use physical violence.

The trick to being okay with using violence is to make sure that you exhaust all other possible avenues for resolving the situation. If the other person continues to push things, then it's on them, not you.

Just knowing your actions will be morally and lawfully justified can help spur you into action in the first place, but we will talk about that in a moment.

For now, know that in order to deal with violence and violent people, you must be confident enough to assert yourself when you have to. Just asserting yourself in a calm and reasonable manner can sometimes be enough to influence the other person into backing down.

Self-assertion is a skill like any other, and therefore needs to be practiced. You can do so in the gym by doing drills.

Have a partner play the part of an aggressor. His job is to try and bully and intimidate you through aggressive dialogue and body language. It is your job to not be intimidated by this, to assume a confident demeanour through body language and calm but assertive dialogue while also making sure to control your personal space well. The more you do these types of drills, the better you will get at asserting yourself and the more confident you will become in general.

Most importantly, you will find it easier to hold your

bottle when you need to.

Non-Violent Postures

The most effective way to exert situational control over a situation is through the use of the fence, a concept most of you should be very familiar with by now.

For those who are not, the fence is fundamentally a way for you to control your personal space and prevent an aggressor from entering into that personal space.

The fence is a difficult concept to explain with just words. Essentially you are adopting and open-handed fighting stance, with the hands held high above those of your aggressor. This allows you to control your space. It also allows you to strike from a good position if need be and adopt a default position very quickly if caught off guard by your aggressor.

Physically speaking there are quite a few different variations on the fence position. The type of fence used depends on the person using it and the circumstances in which it is being used. In general though, whatever type of fence you use, it should be non-aggressive, since the object is to de-escalate rather escalate (unless escalation is your goal, which can work in some cases).

What I am most interested in for this article is the psychology behind the fence concept. By standing firm and not allowing the other guy to get close to you, you are communicating calm and confidence through your body language and tone of voice.

Think of it as drawing a line in the sand. By doing so you are telling the other guy that you will be reasonable with him but if he pushes things too far then you will, without hesitation, use violence to resolve the matter.

That should be your intention at this stage: to avoid using violence if possible, but if you have to use it you will do so, and do so very fucking scarily. Everything about you must give of that exact intention. This in itself is often enough to make the other guy back off.

Pattern Disruption

By asserting yourself in this way you are also disrupting the other guy's pattern. Let me explain that.

Most violent types tend to stick to the same patterns of behaviour when victimising someone. They will approach everyone in the same way, use the same words and phrases, and adopt the same body language, all of which goes to make up a pattern of attack that they know, from experience, works very well for them.

The success of that pattern of behaviour is also dependent on the victim being drawn into the aggressor's reality, so that the victim ends up being controlled like a puppet, reacting in just the same predictable ways in which the aggressor wants them to, which usually means they become intimidated and scared, victims of their aggressor's will.

By exerting situational control from the get-go, you are effectively disrupting that well-worn pattern of behaviour. Just by stepping back into some kind of fence position and saying to your aggressor, "*Wow, hold on a minute mate. Don't come any closer. Stay there and I'll talk to you*", you are throwing a spanner in the works and messing up your aggressor's plan of attack. They now have to re-think their strategy, which is often just too much trouble and they will go find someone else who maybe won't disrupt their plan as much.

Disrupt your aggressor's pattern as quickly as possible and don't allow yourself to get locked into his reality.

I teach people to use their peripheral vision when they are using the fence. I find if you look straight into your aggressor's eyes it is too easy to get locked into their reality. Intimidation sets in quickly and before you know it, you've lost your bottle and he's controlling you instead of the other way around.

So when fencing, get used to looking out of the corner of your eye, rather than directly at your aggressor. This will help you stay calm and detached. You will also pick up movement quicker since the brain interprets peripheral vision signals faster than focused vision signals. If you read my e-book, you will find drills in there to help you develop your peripheral vision.

So by taking control of the situation in the way that you have, you can much more effectively employ a verbal de-escalation strategy or a pre-emptive striking strategy, things you wouldn't be able to do if you were locked into your aggressor's reality and they had control of the situation.

8 GET FIT

"If you don't exercise, put the Twinkie down and get off your ass." **Kelly McCann**

If Combatives is all about preparedness, it makes sense that that preparedness carries over into your physical or combative conditioning. But what is considered adequately fit in relation to defending yourself in a street fight? There are different opinions on this, so let's examine them now.

There are those who believe that physical fitness does not matter much when it comes to self defence because self defence techniques are supposed to incapacitate an attacker so quickly that fitness becomes irrelevant.

That may be true in an ideal world, but we don't live in an ideal world, so that viewpoint is a little naive and maybe even dangerous. In my experience, street fights don't usually go down the way you expect them too. Unexpected variables always come into play to mess up your perfect game plan and often times, the quick finish you were hoping for eludes you and you end up in a protracted brawl.

As Kelly McCann has said, you can't depend on technique, power and luck all aligning perfectly to create a guaranteed outcome. Remember what I said before: there are no guarantees in self defence, so you shouldn't expect them. Neglecting your combative conditioning completely is therefore folly and could get you in serious trouble.

Those who take the middle ground on this issue believe that physical fitness is a requirement of good self defence, and these people generally achieve this level of fitness in their own way, through running or weight training or through some kind of cross training program.

This level of fitness will get you through most self defence situations, which is why most Combatives practitioners tend to settle for this middle ground.

The ideal level of fitness to have would be higher again, putting you in peak physical condition. It takes a lot of training and dedication to get to this stage though, and not everyone will achieve that. It largely depends on your overall goals when it comes to self defence, how dedicated you are and how much time you can spur.

What is more important is doing the right kind of physical conditioning. You have to look at how most fights go down. They are generally short, brutal affairs as opposed to long drawn out brawls (although these can happen also), so it makes sense to tailor you're conditioning and training to that.

There is also the fact that adrenaline during a fight can drain you of energy very quickly, so it makes sense to allow for this as well.

During an attack you will rely mostly on your fast-twitch muscle fibers for speed, power and explosiveness, so training that will develop these muscle fibers is required. Interval training that consists of short, intense activity is ideal for this. It also would make sense to develop your aerobic endurance to some extent as well, through running or such like.

The Combatives training itself will also help to develop your combative conditioning. Doing lots of pad work and plenty of intense training drills will by themselves, raise your level of conditioning.

It boils down to giving yourself the best chance in any given situation, so the better your combative conditioning, the greater chance you will have should you have to really go for it on the street.

9 DO COMBATIVES TRAINING

"Combatives is what works in a fight." **Dennis Martin**

Combatives, and reality self defence training in general, has become quite a popular pursuit these days. There now exists a plethora of different schools and systems in the world teaching self defence, all with their own particular take on things (although usually, the difference is just in the marketing). For someone who is looking to gain instruction in Combatives, it can get quite confusing and overwhelming trying to find good information and instruction.

Here, I'm going to give you some advice on how to go about finding proper instruction in Combatives and what to look for in an instructor. I'm also going to explain to you how to stand on your own two feet and think for yourself when it comes to learning Combatives and self defence in general.

Firstly, you need to know what you are looking for. A good Combatives system should fulfill the following criteria:

• Basic strikes that will work pre-emptively or defensively
• Natural everyday positions as a starting point for situational control, and which are easy to strike from
• An emphasis on power striking, with heavy impact
• A head-hunting mentality--striking the head wherever possible
• Simple but effective counters to common street attacks
• An emphasis on mindset and the cultivation of ferocious resolve or the willingness to do what it takes to

survive
- Brutal ground fighting techniques
- An emphasis on dirty fighting and tactics
- Skills that will work under high stress conditions
- Stress inoculation training to aid an understanding of stress and how to operate under it

Those are some of the main defining characteristics of a Combatives system. It's a very no nonsense approach to self defence and one you should seek if you want instruction in how to defend yourself.

Try to find an instructor who has some sort of real world experience behind them, such as security work or even military experience. Instructors who have experience in what they are teaching tend to be better instructors because they have been there and know from hard won experience what works and what doesn't in real violent altercations.

As well as this, an instructor should know their subject very deeply, they should understand every single aspect of it and this should be apparent in how they put the material they are teaching across. Avoid instructors who see everything in black and white terms, and who see themselves as being right all the time. A good instructor will change their mind often and re-evaluate things as new information comes along.

Combatives training should be a constant process of discovery, interplay between instructor and student(s). Classes should be fluid, wherein everyone involved is continually re-evaluating, questioning and re-thinking things.

It's a creative process from which everyone benefits. The student gets the best possible instruction and the instructor gains a clearer picture and deeper understanding of what to teach and how to teach it.

More importantly, it's more fun this way. Operating within a rigid, structured program (such as in traditional martial arts) where everything has to be done just so, is not conducive to having fun. And having more fun only aids in the learning process (as we shall see shortly).

Structure can still be present, but it must be loose, not constrictive to the point where it kills creativity or discovery.

That's the kind of class format you should be looking for.

Thinking for Yourself

There are often arguments in the Combatives/SD community, about who is right and who is wrong; about what techniques/concepts/principles/tactics/strategies etc. are right, and which ones are wrong.

The bottom line however, is that anything that leaves you standing and your attacker on the floor unconscious, is good.

Right and wrong do not matter.

How you put the other guy down doesn't matter.

It only matters that you did.

If you say a technique is wrong and someone else uses that same technique to survive a physical confrontation, is that technique (or tactic, strategy…whatever) still "wrong"?

Of course not. How can it be wrong when it was used successfully? Even once.

Just because a technique or way of doing something does not fit your definition of what is right--or even what makes good self defence-- it does not mean that the technique in question is wrong or invalid.

That's just how you perceive things.

There are so many different approaches to self protection because there are so many different people teaching it. What an instructor teaches is just their learning of the subject.

We can put too much stock in instructors-- in what they say and teach. We never seem to look beyond the personality or system and realise that what is being taught is merely one person's experience of a very large and very complex subject.

You would do much better if you became your own instructor and figured out what your particular take on self defence is.

You have to own what you do. You must have your own approach-- not a bad carbon copy of someone else's.

That approach doesn't have to be ground-breaking or new, and can pull from many different sources, but it should fit you perfectly. It should feel natural and flow from you when needed.

To achieve this means taking full responsibility for your own training and not leaving it in the hands of an instructor (however good the instructor). It means thinking critically about everything and going with your gut on what feels right to you.

It means taking proof over opinion and conjecture.

It means testing stuff out until you are satisfied.

You may not become invincible with this approach, but you will certainly increase your chances of survival if the shit hits the fan sometime.

Your self defence is the *only* self defence that works. In my experience, it's the only form of self defence that does the job. Not someone else's take on it.

There is no right or wrong in self defence, not really.

There is only what works for us as individuals, and what doesn't.

So by all means, gain as much instruction as you can (the right instruction, of course), but be aware that the final say rests with you.

The problem with following particular instructors is that you end up putting them on a pedestal and treating them like demi-gods, which can affect your objectivity. Look at what each instructor is teaching, evaluate it and take from them what you think is good and discard the rest (although only after thorough testing, of course).

I'm a big believer in teaching yourself; it's what I've

always done. You will get a deeper understanding of the subject this way, rather than taking things at face value because another instructor says this or that is right or wrong.

Just like in martial arts, Combatives to me is about following your own path, it's a personal journey and the more you think and do for yourself, the more you will get out of it and the better you will be. This understanding, more than anything, has allowed me to make the most progress in my training, and if you follow this credo, so will you.

If you have no wish to go to any classes then your only other option is to do things for yourself. Get hold of some books or DVD's and start to learn the techniques for yourself.

Here are some tips on solo training for self defence.

Solo Training

Don't try to do too much in one session. Pick just a few techniques or drills to work on throughout the session and stick to them. If you try to cover too much you will scatter your focus and end up learning nothing. Remember that good Combatives training is about repetition. To get good you have to train a select few techniques over and over until you master them. If you try to master too many techniques at one time you will end up mastering none.

Train with the street in mind. This means you do not train in a sporting manner. So no shadow boxing or long endurance workouts. Everything you do must be combative, not sporting. Warm up first, then practice your drills and techniques in short bursts. A real street fight is an explosive burst of energy that doesn't last very long. There are no rounds. Only periods of intense combat lasting only several seconds. Your training must reflect that. So basically, go like fuck for no more than ten seconds then stop and repeat.

Add emotional content to your training. Whatever you

do, you must back it up with the correct mindset. If you hit the bag, do so with full intent and aggression. Really imagine that you are in a situation and you have to put this guy down. Anything less will not do. You are practicing accessing state as much as the physical techniques. Hit the switch, go like fuck and then knock the switch off again, making sure to check state every time. Training in this way, you are making sure the techniques will come out under pressure when you need them. This is the only way to train.

Resist the temptation to do long sessions. Long training sessions are for endurance athletes and sport fighters. You will benefit most from shorter sessions of about fifteen to twenty minutes, but train at full intensity during that time. If you feel one session isn't enough, train twice a day.

Here are some suggested solo training drills:

1. Fence And Strike Drill

What's good about this drill is that you don't need any equipment and it can be done anywhere.

Start from a square-on stance, and then move into a fence position with your arms out front as if controlling your space, then from there throw a pre-emptive strike.

Repeat a number of times.

To make the drill more useful, bring your imagination into play. Pretend there is someone in front of you, giving you grief. Control your space as they try to enter it and then, when you think the moment is right, strike with full intent and see yourself knocking the guy out. Remember, emotional content is what makes these techniques stick.

2. Fence, Strike, Blast And Finish

As above, only after you strike pre-emptively you continue to blast your opponent with multiple strikes, moving forward as you do so (forward drive) before finally finishing your opponent off with knees and elbows or some other technique of your choice.

3. Imaginary Brawl Drill

For this drill you are going to be playing out a whole attack scenario from start to finish. Think of a scenario first. You could be walking to your car in a dimly lit car park after a particularly tiring day at work or you could be standing outside the chippy on after having had a few drinks with friends. Whatever. Your imagination is the limit here.

Once you have a scenario in mind, really put yourself into it, mentally and emotionally. Begin to act it out the way a real actor would.

Let's take the car park example. You are walking to your car when you spot two dodgy looking guys loitering near your car. Your spidey sense starts to tingle and you can feel the adrenaline begin to bubble up inside you. Something isn't right (really feel this!). As you continue to walk to your car, one of the guys (dressed in jeans, black jacket and baseball cap) asks you for a light. You tell him you don't have one. No sooner have you answered him when the other guy (wearing track suit bottoms and a dark coloured hoodie) suddenly rushes towards you, drawing his fist back in preparation to hit you. The fight is on.

That's the set up. What way this scenario goes is up to you. The important thing is that you mimic every move as it happens. If you strike one of the guys, then do so for real and really feel the impact. If you get hit or grabbed, react to that for real.

Fall to the floor and grapple. Enact the whole fight. Then when it's over, walk away.

Done right, with your imagination in full swing, this can end up feeling like a real fight. It's almost like visualisation practice but you are physically acting out each movement instead of just picturing it in your head.

Try to be alone when doing this drill. If anyone sees you, they will think you've lost your mind as you throw yourself around and fight imaginary attackers!

10 LEARN TO HIT HARD

"If I had to give someone self defence advice it would be learn to hit fucking hard." **Geoff Thompson**

One of the most fundamental skills to learn in Combatives is the ability to generate powerful strikes that will take an attacker down in the quickest time possible. You may still get away with having little power in your strikes–you may still prevail–but it will take you longer to do so, because you will have to hit your attacker more times in order to put them down.

Having to throw more strikes takes time, and that's time you are giving your attacker to possibly come back at you, or for someone else to join in. No one wants to get involved in protracted fights. Most just want it over and done with in the quickest time possible, and one of the best ways for that to happen is to hit your attacker as hard as you possibly can. This means you have to spend a lot of time on power generation.

Obviously this does not mean that you will drop attackers like flies every single time. It merely means that you have significantly increased your chances of dropping the other guy quickly.

That's reason enough to spend time on power generation, don't you think?

What Is Power?

When we talk about power generation we are really talking about force generation. However, a better way of looking at it would be in terms of momentum, which can be defined as being the product of accelerated mass.

The bigger picture of what you are doing when you strike is that you are accelerating your mass (your body) in the direction of your target (an attacker) in order to create an impact between you (specifically, your hand or fist) and the opposing force (your attackers head).

For this process to occur with maximum effect and efficiency, a number of biomechanical concepts and principles are brought into play.

The scale of impact of your strike is measured against how skillfully you are able to engage this momentum process to full capacity.

Power (momentum) is first generated in the core of your body, as well as with the hips, which will also cause the spine to twist. This is the beginning of a kinetic chain or kinetic link that ends with you throwing the strike. The faster you can engage all the links in the kinetic chain, the more acceleration you will produce and thus the more powerful (forceful) the strike will be.

When looking to generate momentum the larger body parts (hips, abdominals etc.) are the first to move in the sequence, quickly followed by the smaller body parts (arms, hands) that feed of this momentum to produce fast, dynamic movements. This is also known as force summation.

Power is not about pushing of from the ground as some people think. Pushing off from the ground will add weight to your strike, but it won't add velocity.

It is more important to maximize the velocity of the strike than the weight behind it. Weight is still important, but velocity is even more so.

Driving up from the ground will not add to the velocity of the strike because of the direction of the force vector. The force is travelling upwards instead of forwards.

Generating force from the hips/core ensures the velocity travels forward into the strike, which is where it is needed.

The twisting of the leg and foot therefore, is just a by-product of the force generated in the core and through the spine.

Keeping the rear leg weighted behind you, as is the case with the classic boxing mechanics, will not aid velocity. It is much better to allow the rear leg to travel forward with the hips to ensure max velocity and momentum.

Everything has to contribute to the forward momentum in other words. Nothing gets left trailing behind to hinder this process.

To aid balance, you post on the front leg.

The key to this summation of forces is timing. Each link in the kinetic chain must be activated at precisely the right time.

The Stretch Shortening Cycle

Another key factor in power generation is something called the Stretch Shortening Cycle (SSC). This occurs when you quickly stretch a muscle and then just as quickly contract that muscle. This will add a significant amount of elastic energy to your strike.

This is done by simply pulling back and loading the strike. The more distance the striking tool (the hand) has to travel, the more velocity it will gain and thus the more force/impact will be generated.

This obviously raises the issue of telegraphing, which really, is a non-issue, as I've already said in a previous article. At such close range, it matters little if you telegraph the strike for it only takes a split second to do so and it will make little difference in terms of your opponent seeing the strike coming. Loading up in this way however, will make a significant difference in the power of your strike.

The quicker you can stretch and then contract the muscles involved in loading, the more power you will generate.

And speaking of elastic energy...

Plastic And Elastic Energy

The kind of impact you cause with your strike will largely depend on which of these two kinds of energy you use.

Plastic energy is utilised by pushing through your target. Allowing your strike to carry on through your target until it fizzles out, having the effect of sending an attacker flying backwards, may seem like a good thing to do, but it actually isn't in terms of impact. By allowing your strike to carry on unchecked you are giving your attacker the chance to absorb the energy of the strike with 100% of their body mass. In effect, they will absorb what you give them and come right back at you again, since you haven't really done anything to hurt them or cause them any real trauma.

Elastic energy on the other hand, is utilised by allowing the striking hand to bounce back of the target naturally using the recoil generated by the impact. The effect will then be that your attacker will absorb all of the impact in a concentrated area of their body (the head), which will have a much greater traumatic effect on them because it will rattle their brain more inside their skull.

Care must be taken not to pull the strike too soon, as this will impede the energy transference of the strike. Follow through with the strike and allow the hand to bounce back naturally. It takes some practice to get this right, but the effect is well worth it.

The Serape Effect

We also have something called the Serape Effect. The Serape Effect is a band of muscle that criss-crosses the body from opposite shoulder to opposite hip on both sides. It is designed to aid rotational movements in the human body.

Logan and McKinney explain it this way in their book, *The Serape Effect*:

"The serape effect incorporates several major concepts which are vital to the understanding of movement. In ballistic actions such as throwing and kicking, the serape muscles add to the summation of internal forces. They also transfer internal force from a large body segment, the trunk, to relatively smaller body parts, the limbs. For

example, the serape effect functions in throwing [striking] by summating, adding to, and transferring the internal forces generated in the lower limbs and pelvis to the throwing limb."

Speaking of a right-handed thrower (substitute "thrower" for "striker"–the movements are much the same), Logan and McKinney state:

"There is a definite interaction between the pelvic girdle on the left and the throwing limb on the right by way of concentric contraction of the left internal oblique, right external oblique, and serratus anterior on the right at the initiation of the throw. The pelvic girdle is rotating to the left and the rib cage is rotating to the right."

This means we should base our strikes around rotational movements, as opposed to linear ones.

So as you throw the strike you shouldn't just be thrusting directly forward, but down and across to match the pulling movements of the muscles connecting from the left hip to the right shoulder. As you do this, you will notice the left hip rotating to the left and the tension in the left ribcage as it pulls in and rotates to the right. These movements together will combine to aid in your explosive power generation.

So basically, as you throw the strike, you are angling downwards to match the natural movements involved in this Serape Effect. I hope this makes sense, because it is very important.

If you were to throw a right palm strike, you would not just be thrusting forward with it in a linear fashion, but rotating your whole body to the left and downwards slightly at the same time, posting on the left leg to aid balance and allowing the right leg to come forward to aid momentum.

Head movement also comes into play here as well. For a right handed strike, the head will fly forwards and to the left to allow the body to rotate forwards.

This does not mean that all you have to do is throw your head quickly forwards to do a powerful strike. The head movement is more of a by-product of all the other movements involved, just as the leg and foot twist is a by-product also.

Other Factors

In order for power to occur, we have established that you must move your mass as quickly as possible with maximum velocity to the target.

For this to be effective however, you must also present a solid structure to resist the recoil that will come from the impact. A weak structure will result in a weak transference of force and the energy you generated will end up going back into you again.

Strength is another factor effecting power. The use of strength should not be your initial concern when striking. Your initial concern should be correct body mechanics and transference of power. Once that is accomplished, you can then add in your strength to the equation, using it just at the end of the process to gain added force and impact.

You can also gain further momentum by stepping quickly forward with your lead leg, but this is obviously only possible when you have the space to do so.

There will also be times when you are unable to utilise the full kinetic chaining process, because you may be in an awkward position or completely lacking in space. In this case, you would then use your spine to generate power. It is possible to generate tremendous power with just the spine alone. When you see someone strike almost casually with little movement to affect a great impact, they are doing so by using the spine, twisting it very rapidly and forcefully.

(You can practice this by placing your open hand very close to a focus mitt so you can practice delivering impact at very short distances, without using your body much, except the spine. You'll be surprised by how much impact you can generate.)

Inner-power, generated by emotion, can also be helpful in hitting hard. Aggression, anger etc. will help fuel your physical movements. I talked about this in another article.

Finally, relaxation is also a key factor to power generation. Tension will decrease your potential velocity in two ways:

1. You have to overcome the force of the muscles that are tense (this is how most beginners strike – they are very stiff).

2. You can't stretch the muscle to use the SSC, since it's impossible to stretch a contracted muscle.

You must therefore learn to fire of only the muscles needed to do the job, and relax the opposing muscles.

Explosiveness

Biomechanical technique is only half the story when it comes to hitting hard.

Technique is important, but what's even more important for a strike to reach its full potential, is explosiveness. You must be able to load up your strike with explosive energy, and reload it just as quick, repeating the process as many times as you have to, something that Steve Morris calls the "Uzi Effect", likening the process to the rapid and continuous firing of a submachine gun.

For a strike to be truly effective, you must also be able to engage this process at the drop of a hat, without any preparedness whatsoever. There is no time in fighting to ready yourself. There is no cocking of the gun before you shoot. You just shoot. That's it.

There is definitely an art to throwing a great strike, one that is effortless and devastating at the same time, and this aspect is often lost on those who try to reduce striking (or any other technique for that matter) to simple mechanics without any consideration for the deeper aspects that go into it.

It's almost ironic that the martial arts are called such, for they spend more time teaching people how to move like robots, how to perform in an unnatural manner, instead of stressing natural movement and unique personal input from the practitioner (the art). The same thing exists in self protection, where every technique is boiled down to simple mechanics, but with a bit more emphasis on mindset and "violent intent".

When technique is stressed above all else, you turn a person into a robot, one who can perform moves that are identical to the ones in the instruction manual. This kind of learning goes against the very personal nature of real learning. In real learning you do not simply copy what someone else is doing, but instead you express the specific movements in your own way. Learning a technique should therefore not just be a process of replication. It should also be about creating as much energy as possible from nothing, and efficiently and explosively directing that energy to a very precise area outside of yourself, which in this case would be your opponent. You can't learn to do that just by concentrating on technique alone. Or as athletics coach Vernon Gambetta puts it in an article from his excellent *Functional Path Training* blog:

"The body is so efficient and remarkable in its ability to solve complex movement problems. It just never ceases to surprise me, in many ways it is predictably unpredictable in its ability to adapt. The body is not a machine constructed of interchangeable parts, it a kinetic chain consisting of interdependent links that work in harmony to reduce and produce force in reaction to gravity and the ground. In coaching to refine human motion we must stress connections, linkages, coordination and rhythm. This allows the body to work its magic, produce the poetry of motion that allows it to self-organize and solve complex movement problems. The human body has the remarkable ability to produce finely tuned movements that in the initial stages of learning appear uncoordinated and disjointed but through error detection and subsequent correction discard what does not work and refine and perfect what does work. So coaching is learning to guide, to direct and sometimes to stay out of the way and allow the wisdom of the body take over and be confident in our guidance."

There are also other factors that you must consider if you want to increase the explosiveness of your strikes. Let's look at those other factors now.

Internal And External Focus

Where you put your focus as you do a strike is important. If you over-obsess about your technique and your focus is largely on the mechanics of your strike, where you are concentrating on getting the moves right, then you are focusing internally, and your strike will not flow as it should, which also means it won't be very explosive either.

Another important point to bear in mind is that pausing to think about what you are about to do, and keeping your main focus on just your movements, you are giving your Golgi Tendon Organs time to perform their inhibitory function, which will result in less muscle contraction, which obviously will affect the explosiveness of your strike.

To overcome this you should switch to a more external focus with your strike. In other words, your focus should be on the effect you want your strike to have. If want to hit your opponent hard in the head, then that's what your concentration should be on– the target in front of you.

Having such an external focus takes your focus out of yourself and on to your opponent, allowing your movements to be much more fluid and natural. Your focus is only on hitting your opponent however hard, not on how you are going to do that.

You can test this approach yourself. Simply strike a focus pad or bag with your focus on the movements of what you are doing. You may find yourself almost locking up slightly, over controlling and pulling the strike. Your movements will feel unnatural and lacking in spontaneity. Now put your focus only on the pad and hitting it as hard as you can. Give no thought to your movements, on whether you are doing them right or wrong. Just do. You should find your strikes to be much more explosive and spontaneous. You may also be surprised at how much more impact you can generate with your strike.

It doesn't matter that your technique is not exactly as you've been taught it by someone else. It's the effect of a movement that is important, not the movement itself. Measure your techniques in terms of effectiveness, not in terms of some biomechanical or aesthetic ideal.

Rate Coding

Rate coding refers to the frequency that your brain sends messages telling a muscle to contract. The faster the frequency the greater the intensity of any given muscular contraction.

Rate coding appears to be highly related to the excitability of the central nervous system (CNS). A highly excited CNS can produce greater force at a faster rate due to the positive impact on rate coding.

This factor is also known as the Psycho Factor because it is inherently influenced by the psychological state. To have a positive impact on rate coding that will increase the explosiveness and power of your strike, you must be able to excite your CNS enough, which means you must be able to psych yourself up at a seconds notice, without any build up at all.

Adrenaline will obviously do the job of exciting your CNS and improving rate coding, which is why you are always faster, stronger and more powerful when adrenaline or nervous energy is in your system.

You can't really rely on an outside stimulus to trigger excitement in your nervous system however. You must be able to excite your own CNS at will, to generate explosive power and energy from nothing.

How naturally excitable your CNS is, is actually one of those intangible factors that separate why some people seem to be able to really fly and others struggle. The natural high flyers have a CNS that is simply more excitable and as such they are able to more readily turn on their muscles and generate power.

To improve rate coding you can practice an exercise

called the Stimulation Method. Here you perform one exercise to really activate or excite the CNS. You then follow it up with an exercise to take advantage of the CNS excitability, which temporarily boosts rate coding. Gradually your body becomes more sensitive to the neural discharges from your CNS and learns to accept a new level of force as being normal for a particular movement. For striking purposes, you could therefore practice throwing a medicine ball or performing the striking movement with a dumbbell first of all, to excite the CNS, before training the strike without weight, taking advantage of the boost in rate coding.

Relaxation

Obviously relaxation is going to play a role here, as it does in most other aspects of training. It stands to reason that the more relaxed your muscles are before you fire them, the more explosive you are going to be.

Learning to stay relaxed will also aid in helping to

reduce the reflex action of the Golgi Tendon Organ, which I mentioned earlier.

The same goes for your mind. Learn to stay mentally relaxed as well.

Exercises To Improve Explosiveness

Plyometric exercises are good for building up power and explosive force in the body, with exercises like

clapping push ups or sit-ups while throwing a medicine ball.

You can also throw a medicine ball at the wall as hard as you can to develop power, making sure to keep the movements similar to when you are striking.

Also practice just exploding into your strike every time you do it, especially in an internal sense.

It's all about exciting the CNS, and to do that you need as much emotional content behind what you do as possible. Fill your strikes with hate, anger or whatever emotion or emotions most drive you. Every time you practice a strike you are not just practicing, you are engaging an opponent. Thinking in this way will help you explode into the strike more.

11 TAP YOUR AGGRESSION

"In a self protection context, learning to use your aggression is an essential key to success." **Neal Martin**

In our society, aggression is not really prized as one of the more noble qualities in the human race, yet it exists and has existed since we started living and breathing on this planet. It has fuelled countless wars amongst us, both on a massive scale and also on a smaller, more interpersonal one. Most people don't like aggression in any of its forms, yet it is always there in all of us, ready to be used at any time.

Aggression is a form of energy, and like any energy, it is neither positive nor negative. All energy is neutral. Only our actions can be judged positive or negative. It is up to you to use the energy you have in the most responsible way you can.

So aggression is neither to be feared nor frowned upon. It is merely energy that you can use to help manifest your desires. If you decide to use that energy to unjustifiably hurt another human being, then that it is up to you. That's on you. You may have used aggression to help you hurt that person, but aggression did not create the desire to do so in the first place.

You cannot blame your aggression when you cross the line. The blame lies with you for not being able to control it.

Aggression can be used in a very positive sense, especially when it comes to self protection. In a physical altercation, aggression, properly used, is one the most powerful weapons you have at your disposal. It cannot be underestimated how powerful an energy source aggression can be. To put it mildly, it can really pull you out of hole.

What Is Aggression Exactly?

Wikipedia defines aggression in the following way:

"Aggression, in its broadest sense, is behaviour, or a disposition, that is forceful, hostile or attacking. It may occur either in retaliation or without provocation. In narrower definitions that are used in social sciences and behavioural sciences, aggression is an intention to cause harm or an act intended to increase relative social dominance. Predatory or defensive behaviour between members of different species may not be considered aggression in the same sense. Aggression can take a variety of forms and can be physical or be communicated verbally or non-verbally."

There can be a number of causes to this behaviour. One theory suggests that aggression is biological, that it is built into us a species, similar to the hunger and sex drives. There may be truth in this, given how much aggressive drive and behaviour has shaped human history, and how aggression seems to exist just as prevalently in the animal kingdom as it does in the human one.

The theory also suggests that this biological drive causes a build-up of energy in us that can only be released by "catharsis", or a release of emotional tension. Again, this release can result in either negative (hurting someone) or positive (channelled) action.

Other theories on aggression suggest that it is more of a learned response, more so than a biological one. We learn to be aggressive by watching others be aggressive, and if this aggressive behaviour results in a reward of some kind, then we adopt it even more. This is part of our social conditioning to a large extent. If the environment we grow up in is a particularly aggressive one, then we will naturally learn to use aggression to your own ends, especially against those who are less familiar with aggression.

Another theory, called Negative Affect Theory, proposes that negative feelings and experiences are the main cause of anger and angry aggression. Sources of that behaviour may include pain, frustration, crowding, sadness or depression. Thus we may walk around taking our aggression on other people, as a means of directing the bad feeling away from ourselves. It is also the cause of much of the violence in our society, as we displace our aggression on to one another.

The truth about aggression is wrapped up within all of these theories however. Aggression cannot be narrowed down to a single point of origin. It may be there on a biological level to begin with, but we also learn to use our aggression by watching others do it, and we also fall victim to feelings of angry aggression due to negative thought processes and negative behaviour patterns.

Finding Your Aggression

In a self protection context, learning to use your aggression is an essential key to success. Most people can find the aggression within themselves quite easily, but a surprising number of people cannot. It always interests me when I first take a new student, to see how easily they can rouse the aggression within themselves. Some people really struggle with it.

Being able to tap into and use your aggression, turning it on and off at will, is a skill like any other, and like any skill, it takes a bit of time to master. It's just one of those things that is cultivated through the right training over a long period of time.

In a more immediate sense however, there are things you can do, physical and mental drills, that will help facilitate the longer term process.

In a mental sense, you can start by thinking of things that will naturally arouse your sense of aggression, things that may make you angry even. This kind of thinking will drag the raw aggression to the surface so you can start to work with it and get a feel for it. Notice how it makes you feel in every sense, and try to feel the energising power of it. You can also take this a stage further by doing focused visualisation drills.

Now you can do some physical drills, a good one being what I call simply the aggression drill, where you stand in front of a heavy bag or pad and a partner holds you around the waist. On the go signal you lay into the bag or pad with everything you've got while the person holding you around your waist adds resistance by puling you backwards, forcing you into really driving forward. The only way you will reach the bag or pad and hit with power is if you use aggression to fuel your actions.

Controlling And Using Aggression

Being able to tap into your aggression is all well and good, but if you don't know how to control and channel that energy it can feel a little like you're a trainee Ghostbuster who's just wielded a Proton Pack for the first time–it can be hard to control the stream.

To properly control and channel aggression you must become adept at switching it on and off at will so that you have complete control over it, no matter your physical or mental state.

Remember: aggression is just a form of energy. Certain mental and physical states are just ways to initially find your way to that source of energy. Once you can tap the source without the need for catalysts, you will gain instant access to it at any time. And like everything, the more you use this ability, the stronger and more powerful it gets.

Uncontrolled aggression is not really what you are after in a self protection context (nor indeed, in any fight context) simply because it will largely control you and dictate your behaviour and actions, instead of the other easy around.

Many SP instructors can be heard telling their students to tap into their inner animal and go fucking nuts in a self defence situation, but to me, this is just too over-simplistic to be of any real use to you. Going apeshit in a fight may win you the fight, but it may also make you take things too far, to your detriment. Skill would also go out the window to a great extent, making you vulnerable to some who knows how to fight.

Fair enough if your back is really up against the wall and you need that added energy you get from getting really mad to get you out of trouble, but that's it. In the main, relinquishing control to your inner animal isn't a good idea in a lot of cases.

I've seen the red mist come down over a lot of people and it usually aint pretty to watch. It's also hard to come down from if rage or extreme anger is the driving force behind the aggression. It inevitably gets displaced everywhere.

Cold and controlled aggression is much easier to work with. In this case, the energy is tightly focused and contained, directed only at the threat before you and used in a fairly controlled manner (I say fairly because a lot of time you can't help losing your temper in a fight—you're being hit after all!).

Controlled aggression is a powerful force indeed, and it will make whatever strike you do very powerful also. The trick is channelling your aggression into your movements, something that will only come with deep practice over time.

You must get a deep kinaesthetic sense of your aggression, of how it feels in your body and mind. It is that kinaesthetic representation that you want to create before you strike. Through continued practice you are essentially anchoring that feeling and/or visual representation every time you draw upon your reserves of aggression. This anchor will then be used to trigger your explosive action each time.

The bigger the jolt of aggressive energy you can generate, the more explosive and the more powerful your strikes will be.

On top of this, you must also be conditioned enough, in a physical sense, to sustain this aggression over time.

The more aggressive you are the more energy you will burn and the more lactic acid you will build up in your muscles. You must therefore work on increasing the threshold of your lactic acid system through continued physical conditioning exercises.

The energy of cold aggression will also affect your mindset. It will make you naturally more inclined to press forward and attack your attacker. Sustained, controlled aggression can help you overcome even the most difficult of opponents. It definitely won't make you unbeatable or any such nonsense, but it will make you a force to be reckoned with. Whether that force is enough to overcome your circumstances is another matter entirely, and will depend on your skill as a fighter, the extent of the danger you are facing and a large dose of luck as well.

Like I often say, there are no magical solutions in self defence and aggression is no magical solution either. It is just another tool to help stack the odds in your favour.

Beyond Self Protection

In a personal development sense, it doesn't hurt to learn to cultivate your aggression and channel it into the pursuit of your goals in life. I'm not saying you have to turn into some arrogant corporate go-getter, but to go after your goals with verve and aggressively follow up on whatever opportunities come your way.

When times get tough, as they inevitably will in the pursuit of anything worthwhile in life, and you are met with seemingly insurmountable obstacles, channelled aggression can really help you get fired up enough that you will be able to overcome whatever blocks to your advancement that come up.

Aggression is an energy source, and a powerful one at that. You would do well to learn to tap into that energy source and to further use it in any positive way you can, be it either in protecting yourself.

12 LEARN TO HIT FIRST WHEN NECESSARY

"Hit first. Hit hard."

A common remark I often hear from people who are interested in or train in some kind of self defence is that they just don't have it in them to hit first– to pre-emptively strike a would-be attacker.

This unwillingness to take pre-emptive action is very serious. Not only does it put you at a severe disadvantage-- tactically speaking-- in a physical confrontation, but it also betrays the fact that you have underlying issues that need to be dealt with (such as fear and lack of confidence).

If you happen to be one of those people who "just doesn't have it in them to hit first", and if I was a more brutal type of guy, I'd just tell you straight, "Man the fuck up and just do what has to be done!"

I'm only brutal when you cross me, however. The rest of the time I'm a gentle soul, so I'm going to take a slightly more sensitive approach and do my best to help you clear this thing up once and for all.

Seriously though, you need to get over that shit quick. Your lack of assertiveness makes you look weak, especially in the eyes of the psychopathic thug who wants to rip your face off. A physical confrontation is no place to be a shrinking violet.

Shrinking violets get trampled by violence.

But Neal, you may be saying now. It's not my fault, I can't help it…I just can't throw that first punch and I don't know why!

If you don't know why, you obviously haven't done enough searching for answers. If you haven't done enough searching and trying to get to the bottom of why you can't act pre-emptively, even knowing the full scale of the problem, then you are not serious about your personal safety. Neither are you serious about developing a combative mind, so to speak.

There is also another problem– the problem of credibility. If you are not prepared to do what it takes, what else are you not prepared to do? What is the point of training in self defence at all if you are not prepared to do what it takes?

I used to have the same problem, you know. Suffice to say I got over it. I did what I had to do to fix it. I was motivated to do so. I had no choice since I was working as a doorman at the time.

Don't go thinking now that just because you don't have the same motivation that I had, that you don't have to worry about it.

You do have to worry about it. It will leave you very vulnerable in a number of ways if you don't get it sorted.

So let's start by defining the problem here. The problem is that for some reason you can't pre-emptively strike another person, even if that person is about to strike you. That's the problem—you can't take the initiative and hit first

So what reasons do you have for this unwillingness or inability to act (besides the usual fear that accompanies any physical confrontation, and of course, social conditioning)?

Legal Concerns

Sorry, but no. That's not a reason. We should all be very clear on the fact that the law allows us to pre-emptively strike another person if we are acting on the belief that we are about to be attacked, and that if we have exhausted all other possibilities, hitting first is an acceptable course of action.

You should be clear on the law. You certainly shouldn't fear it, not when it comes to defending yourself from harm. Read up on the law, know what you can and can't do and do your best to stay within the law, but not at the expense of your life.

Fear

This is the most used excuse for lack of action--fear. But fear of what exactly?

The fear of hurting the other guy? That's pretty astonishing, considering the other guy is about to hurt you. Yet I know this fear exists because I used to have it myself. I got rid of it by accepting the fact that it was me or them. That's pretty much all there is to that one.

The fear of making the other guy mad? Newsflash: He's already fucking mad! Would he be trying to launch an assault on you if he were not mad at you for something? No, he wouldn't! Will you make him even madder by hitting him? What does it matter? He's going to hit you no matter what anyway. At least if you get one good shot in before he does, you'll more than likely end the confrontation right there.

If you don't get that first shot in, you're going to be on the back foot and that's never really an ideal place to be in a brutal assault. You'll take damage, sometimes a lot of damage. You may even lose your life.

Oh, but I forgot, your defence is pretty good, right?

Good Defences

There is no such thing as good defence. It is never good to defend in a fight. You should always be attacking in some way. Defending means you are losing, temporarily or not. You're still taking a risk that your defensive skills will work. Given how unpredictable an attacker can be, how surprising they can be in strength and aggression and sheer violent intent, it is asking quite a lot for you to deal with that and do so without taking any damage.

And do I need to remind you that action will always beat reaction? Why go against the math? It doesn't make sense.

Defence is still needed, but in the right circumstances, not because it is the only option you have.

This isn't Hollywood. Defending against a determined attacker is very difficult indeed. If you don't believe me then get some protective gear on and try to defend against some full contact attacks. You'll quickly see how difficult it is.

So those are the main reasons why you think you don't have it in you to hit first. You obviously must know by now that your self protection game-plan is not a sound one.

Let me remind you of a few things. Hitting first in a physical confrontation will give you the best chance of ending that confrontation, with no damage to you and possibly less damage to the other guy. If you'd gotten into a brawl, you could have ended up seriously injuring the guy, maybe even killing him. Not to mention the fact that third parties could have gotten involved while you were distracted and indisposed. The consequences are many.

More than that though, you're inability to hit first is creating a weakness in you that will detract from your confidence and leave you vulnerable. Knowing, or just believing, that you have the ability to hit first will greatly increase your confidence, which will positively affect the way in which you deal with confrontation.

You will feel calmer, more in control, to the point where you are better equipped to de-escalate the situation through a combination of assertiveness and the confidence that comes from knowing that you can end things at any time.

That's very empowering. It's a true combative mind.

Now let's look at the steps you have to take in order to banish this unwillingness once and for all. (And by the way, if you don't do all these steps to completion you might as well give up self defence training and go do something else instead, for you will just be kidding yourself. Despite what you think, you will not be fully equipped to handle a real physical confrontation. And if you think I'm being too blunt, you will have proved my point.)

Step One: Do Your Homework

The first thing you have to do is look at the evidence supporting the use of pre-emptive action. You must clearly see that wherever possible, hitting first is the wisest course of action there is. Find out for yourself why this is so. Think about it logically, do the math and you will see why pre-emption is the best strategy. Look at the anecdotal evidence as well. Talk to people who have used pre-emptive action and find out there experience of it.

Gather all the facts and look at them in the cold light of day, then let them back up your conviction that pre-emptive action is the best course of action in most cases.

Step Two: Make The Decision

Now you have to make a firm decision that you will adopt this strategy of pre-emption, that it will now be your first course of action should you find yourself facing a would-be attacker.

You have to commit yourself to this. You should have worked out in your head, after weighing up all the evidence in the first step, why you need to do this, why you must persist with this strategy

Commit yourself and tell yourself that there is no turning back now. Read the quote below from Goethe, it is one of my favourites and sums things up nicely:

"Until one is committed, there is hesitancy, the chance to draw back— Concerning all acts of initiative (and creation), there is one elementary truth that ignorance of which kills countless ideas and splendid plans: that the moment one definitely commits oneself, then Providence moves too. All sorts of things occur to help one that would never otherwise have occurred. A whole stream of events issues from the decision, raising in one's favour all manner of unforeseen incidents

and meetings and material assistance, which no man could have dreamed would have come his way. Whatever you can do, or dream you can do, begin it. Boldness has genius, power, and magic in it. Begin it now."

Step Three: Train With The Goal In Mind

So you've done your research, you've made the decision to commit to pre-emptive action should the need arise; now you must focus your training around this strategy.

Basically, this means that you must practice being pre-emptive in your training. It means practicing your pre-emptive strikes over and over, to the point where you are completely comfortable using them. You must develop total confidence in each of your strikes.

Take two to three strikes at most and drill the hell out of them. Get each strike totally right. Work on the body mechanics so you get the most power behind each strike. You must be confident that your strikes will do the job, that they will knock a would-be attacker out cold.

You also have to practice scenarios where you strike first. There are plenty of pre-emptive striking drills in my free Combatives Drills e-book, the link for which is in the resources section of this book.

Start with a partner who is being verbally aggressive while holding up the focus pad. Practice striking at the right moment.

From there, move on to full pressure testing. Have a partner wear a helmet and have him go at you with full aggression so you can practice striking with (almost) full power. The more you do these types of drills the more comfortable you will get with pre-emptive striking.

Feel the confidence you get from these drills. Anchor it and let that confidence fuel your actions every time.

Step Four: Believe You Are That Person

Self-belief is important. Look at the kind of person you

need to be in order to use pre-emptive action. What attributes do you need? What kind of mindset do you need?

You should discover most of this while you are doing the training drills. Take how you are doing the drills and believe that you can carry this through to real life if need be.

Think of all this as a journey of self-discovery, for that is exactly what it is. To get to the bottom of your problem you must know yourself, what fears you have, what holds you back, what really motivates you.

Combatives training is the best way to do this. You will not find what you are looking for by doing typical martial arts training. You must push yourself more than that allows.

Remember that no one has the right to attack you in any way, and that you have every right to stand up for yourself. Why would you let some twat get the better of you when it is within your power to put the guy in his place, to put him down, before he gets the chance to hurt you or your loved ones?

These people want to hurt you. Be clear on that. They wouldn't be accosting you if they didn't.

It's you or them. That's the bottom line, my friend.

When all is said and done there is no excuse for castrating yourself by taking your most effective self protection strategy out of play for flimsy reasons.

Grow a pair and stand up for yourself, and don't let fear undermine your personal safety.

13 SELF DEFENCE AND THE LAW

"Legitimate use of violence can only be that which is required in self defense." **Ron Paul**

In this age of extreme political correctness and litigation, the law has essentially become the second enemy as far as self defence goes, and potentially it could inflict a lot more damage on you than any attacker on the street. The days of punching someone to the ground and walking away with no fear of the law getting involved are over. These days, everyone runs to the cops, or some other third party gets the law involved. This is just one more reason why you should do all you can to avoid violent conflict. The paperwork afterwards, even you were justified in your actions, is a nightmare.

This is why is pays to know the basic ins and outs of self defence law. The particulars will vary from country to country and from state to state, but the essentials remain the same, so let's take a quick look at those essentials now. (Note: The following points are a brief summary of the information contained in Rory Miller's *Facing Violence* book. If you want more detailed explanations then read the book. It's a good book and an excellent introduction to the softer skills of self defence. I highly recommend it if you haven't already read it.)

Force Justification

If you were involved in a violent incident where you had to use force then in the eyes of the law you must be able to articulate why you saw the person as a threat and how you knew it. "I had a feeling about the guy" just won't cut it in court. To be a valid Threat an individual must exhibit four things:

1. Intent:
The Threat must indicate that they want to harm you. How did you know? What was the Threat doing or how where they behaving to make you think they were going to attack you (remember threat recognition and pre-contact cues?)?

2. Means:
The means to carry out intent. Basically, if a person has arms and legs then they have the means to carry out an attack.

3. Opportunity:
The Threat must be able to reach you with the means. If they are on the other side of a door then they don't have the opportunity to reach you.

4. Preclusion:
You must convince the court that you did not have any other viable option. You couldn't leave, couldn't talk your way out, you couldn't call for help. You must articulate why force was the one option that would safely work.

Scaling Force
A force incident may change quickly. If IMO are lost then you are no longer defending yourself and you are using excessive force. If you could safely leave and you don't then you have shattered your affirmative defence. For instance, if some guy in a bar tries to pick a fight with you and you had the opportunity to walk away, but instead bit back and got involved in a fight, in the eyes of the law, that's not self defence, that's just fighting.

If you happen to be ambushed then a high level of force is justified as you don't have time to gather enough information to gauge a proper response.

Articulation

We talked about articulation earlier in the book. You must be able to explain each element of your defence: Intent, Means, Opportunity and Preclusion. You must also do so in a clear and logical fashion.

In other wards you must adopt a professional attitude and keep the emotion out of it. "The bastard deserved what he got..." just won't do you any favours in front of a judge and jury.

My Own Views On Self Defence Law

A consensus has formed in the self protection industry and that consensus is this: The law matters more than your own personal safety. It is therefore prudent to think of the law before you think of your own personal safety, even if the law hampers your efforts to keep yourself safe from harm.

Or to put it another way: You just got your head handed to you on a plate by some psychopathic thug, but at least you didn't break any laws in the process.

You may think I'm being over simplistic here, but the fact is I'm not.

It's really very simple: You cannot adequately defend yourself in a violent confrontation while thinking of the law at the same time. In a self defence situation, especially in a very serious one where you stand to get badly injured or killed unless you act with full violent capacity, you must do what you have to in order to survive.

Even if that means acting outside the current self defence laws.

It's ridiculous that you tell someone they must take one for the team, so to speak. Why should anyone open themselves up for physical abuse or death just to stay in line with the rules of a corrupt system that doesn't give a shit about them at the end of the day?

Oh here we go, another macho rant from one of the

"better to be judged by twelve than carried by six" brigade...

It's not like that at all. I'm not so irresponsible to be so blasé about the law. I'm also not so irresponsible to be so blasé about violence either, which is kind of the point of this article.

Yeah well, you may be saying now, you won't be saying that when you're lying in a jail cell with a guy who has a chin like the Desperate Dan look-a-like in Tango and Cash.

You'd be misunderstanding me if you said that however.

The law is the law. I know that. I have to try and abide by its rules like everyone else. And so do you.

The point is though, I don't need the law to tell me what is right from wrong, just like I don't need any religion to dictate my morals to me.

I, like most other decent people, have an in-built moral compass that works just fine.

I know right from wrong.

I can therefore make justified force decisions. I can trust myself enough to do that, and have done so many times in the past.

I am very aware of the law and what constitutes right and wrong in a situation.

But I will not put lawful considerations above my own personal safety. I will not allow them to hamper my ability to defend myself against someone who is trying to hurt me or my loved ones.

It is simply too risky to err on the side of caution when it comes to defending yourself against a valid physical threat. Such circumstances require no fucking about. Such circumstances require you to get in there and do what you have to do.

And you notice I said "valid" threat? That's because I am not going to use violence against someone unless they intend to use, or are using it, on me or someone I love.

I will satisfy the lawful requirements of intent, means, opportunity and preclusion. I will only use physical violence as a last resort.

And not just because that is the legally right thing to do, but also because it is the morally right thing to do.

When I think about all the legal considerations that go along with defending yourself, I quickly start to feel paralyzed by it all, like I'm caught in a web. I feel like I am giving my power away to the bad guy, handing myself to him on a plate.

That's not a good mindset to have in a self defence situation. That kind of mindset can get you killed.

And what effect will all this legal shit have on actual self defence training in the long run? Will it eventually render self defence training completely inadequate and not up to the job anymore? Will it make people afraid to train in a combatively sound way because they think using certain techniques will land them a prison sentence?

Without combatively sound principles to underpin our training, our training becomes useless and a waste of time. But hey, at least we're abiding by the law...the law that doesn't care about you anyway, just to remind you.

Look, it's like this: when faced with violence you use violence to get you through it, not the law.

When faced with the judicial system, you use the law to get you through it.

It's about keeping things in context.

Yes, the law is a consideration, but by no means the only one.

If you are a basically good, right thinking person, you will understand the concept of reasonable force and you will make right decisions. You don't need to clutter your mind with legalities. You can do that afterwards when you have to justify your actions.

The question of going too far in a violent confrontation is also a moot point to me. I train so I won't go too far. Training gives me self-control. If it didn't, what would be the point in training at all?

If you are not responsible enough to keep yourself from going too far in your use of violence, then you really shouldn't be training in self defence, for you can't handle the power the training gives you.

But don't criticise others who can handle the power that training gives them. Just because you think a technique or fighting method is dangerous, doesn't mean I'm going to kill somebody with it or even use it in an unlawful sense. It also doesn't mean I shouldn't be training it.

I train for every eventuality, and for extreme cases, I train extreme techniques. I am also very aware of the context in which such techniques should be used. I trust myself enough to apply the right response to whatever situation I'm facing, and in all the confrontations I've been in, that's exactly what I did.

You respond as best you can to the threat before you and hope for the best.

If you think you can respond like some mechanical robot, always making just the right moves, then you are sadly mistaken. Violence doesn't work like that, I'm afraid. And if you think that it does, you are only showing your lack of experience in such matters.

Responsible people will always train responsibly. Irresponsible people will always end up in trouble no matter what they do.

The law may be important, but avoiding death or serious injury is even more important.

The law will not help you when you are six feet under or hooked up to a life support machine in a hospital.

Remember that the next time you are facing some slavering psychopath who intends to leave you in a bloody mess.

APPENDIX A

VIOLENT INTENT AND INSTILLING PANIC

"When I fight someone, I want to break his will. I want to take his manhood. I want to rip out his heart and show it to him." **Mike Tyson**

There is a saying that I'm fond of: "Amateurs fight bodies. Professionals fight minds."

Effective self defence is not all about how much bodily damage you can inflict on an attacker. It is also about how much damage you can inflict on them psychologically.

Without the will to back it up, the body is useless. If you take away your attackers will to fight you will leave them with nothing but the sour taste of defeat.

Musashi was a master of this type of psychological beat-down. He employed many tricks to mess with an opponent's head before and during the fight. It was this psychological cunning, backed up with supreme physical skills that made Musashi one of the greatest fighters to ever live.

If you want to be more effective at self defence and be a more superior fighter, then you must find ways in which to instill a sense of panic into your attacker or would-be attacker.

You must find ways to break their will and take away their fighting spirit in order to defeat them.

It's a fact that most people do not like to fight. Physical violence is a scary proposition to most people.

Social violence is motivated by ego and peer pressure

and as such, most of those who instigate social violence would much rather win in a confrontation without fighting. They will try to win by using bullying and intimidation tactics first, only turning to violence if that doesn't work for them.

Resource and process predators want something from you first of all. Violence is just a tool to get that something from you. If they can get it without using violence, all the better for them. Less hassle that way.

My point here is that you should be aware of most people's unwillingness to engage in violence, and that you should learn to take advantage of this unwillingness.

Most people will only fight because they think they have too for whatever reason. They don't really want to be doing it and they will look for a way to disengage as quickly as possible.

By using certain tactics before and during a fight you can take advantage of this inherent weakness in people and force them to confront the hard fact that they were not really up for violence in the first place.

Use the following tactics to break the will of your attacker and force them into disengaging from the fight.

Project Violent Intent

Without a doubt, this is the number one tactic for forcing a would-be attacker into capitulation.

At the pre-fight stage, when a would-be attacker is giving you the interview, you must be able to project enough violent intent that your have-a-go asshole picks up on it and decides that starting a fight with you may not be a good idea after all.

In effect, you must scare him into backing down.

But what exactly is violent intent?

Violent Intent in this context is the PURE will to do harm to another human being by any means necessary. It does not concern itself with the frontal lobe deliberations of how this is best done. It simply desires to cause damage.

Pure violence, in other words.

Or put another way:

Violent Intent only has one question and it isn't "how will I do violence?" but rather an impatient "*when* can I get to do it?"

If you have ever come across a truly psychopathic thug (and I've met a few in my time) you will know why this works. A person of this nature--someone with real violent intent, a truly violent psychopath--is very good at communicating that intent. Just by being in their presence you can pick up on the fact that this person will turn violent at the slightest provocation. They are live wires and unpredictable to boot.

A great example of this kind of personality (disorder) is Begbie in the movie *Trainspotting*, as played by the brilliant Robert Carlyle, who completely nails that role in every respect.

This is exactly how you want a would-be attacker to feel when they try it on with you. You want them to feel like they have perhaps bitten of more than they can chew.

In my early days on the door I didn't really project much in the way of violent intent. Consequently, a lot of people thought they could have a go with me or just refused to acknowledge my authority.

Eventually I realised that you had to adopt a certain attitude when dealing with troublesome punters. They had to believe you would turn on them if they didn't adhere to your instructions. Punters will look for weakness in a doorman when first confronted. If a punter sees any weakness at all they will play on it. You can't give them an inch.

Once I was able to project violent intent from the get go, I got a lot less trouble from punters. When they sensed I was willing to use violence if need be, they invariably backed down and did as they were told.

Here's the thing though: YOU CAN'T FAKE VIOLENT INTENT. YOU MUST MEAN IT.

In other words, you must really be willing to use violence if necessary.

In my experience, just by having the willingness to use violence, your confidence will increase, since you have already made your decision to act if you have too. This increased confidence will add to the potency of your violent intent and thus your would-be attacker will feel it much more keenly and will therefore be more likely to capitulate.

Remember, most people don't want to fight. Be aware of this and use it to manipulate the other person.

Use Overwhelm To Break Your Attackers Will

As I've just said, most people don't want to fight, even when they are fighting. It therefore doesn't take much to get them to capitulate and submit in most cases.

A very effective way to put the fight out of an attacker is to make them feel overwhelmed, physically and psychologically.

In a physical sense you do this by attacking hard and fast and just not letting up until the other guy is down.

Fuel your attack with violent intent and completely shock your attacker into giving up the fight.

A good way to do this is by hitting your attacker from all angles so that he doesn't know where the next strike is coming from. This tends to overwhelm their brain and force them into giving up.

An excellent technique for instilling panic in an attacker is the Shredder technique, as devised by Richard Dimitri. The idea behind the Shredder concept is to completely overwhelm an attacker physically and psychologically. It is a continuous attack on their senses that will very quickly cause the fight to go out of them.

When it comes to the crunch, it really doesn't matter what techniques you use, just as long as your actions are fuelled by violent intent, enough to shock your attacker into giving up.

Apply Forward Pressure

Putting your attacker on the back foot is one of the surest ways in which to instill panic in them.

Once you launch your attack, continue to move forward, railroading through your attacker and don't stop until they hit the ground.

Combined with the previous tactic, this will make your attacker feel even more overwhelmed as they frantically try to regain ground.

The important thing here is that you give them no space in which to manoeuvre so that they find it impossible to regain their position.

Without positioning, they can't fight back.

There is a real sense of panic that comes when someone is constantly pressing forward on you like that and hitting you at the same time. The first instinct is to cover up, which makes fighting back impossible (you can't defend and attack at the same time). It almost feels like you are being pushed towards the edge of a cliff. You panic just as much.

Once again, pure aggression and violent intent should fuel your actions here. The harder and more aggressively you press your attacker back, the more panic you will instill in them and the quicker you will break their will to fight.

Employ Tactical Savagery

Using what Sammy Franco calls Tactical Savagery is another very effective way to instill panic in an attacker.

Tactical Savagery involves using biting, clawing and gouging techniques to make your attacker feel like they are being mauled by some kind of wild animal—which of course they are...you!

These techniques tend to be last resort tactics when you are in a tight spot. I certainly wouldn't recommend biting anyone unless you absolutely had to due to the amount of blood-borne pathogens and diseases present today.

A lot of the time it is enough that your attacker feels like they are being bitten. You don't have to break the skin to do this. You just make a show of biting them without actually doing so.

APPENDIX B

CULTIVATING A PRESENCE OF MIND TO COUNTER-BALANCE FEAR

As human beings we draw a distinction between ourselves and our furry friends in the animal kingdom, thinking of ourselves as rational creatures that, unlike our cuddly cousins, have the ability to think and reason. This is what separates us from other creatures.

Whilst that is true, what really separates us from other creatures on this planet is our ability to feel emotion: to laugh, to cry, to take the piss out of each other when we do stupid things (which is all too often!).

The illusion that we are calm and rationale creatures is maintained throughout our daily lives as we appear to exert control over things.

The reality is however, that we are never far from falling apart at the seams. Place any one of us in an adverse situation and our apparent rationality and self-control goes out the window.

We react to pressure by growing fearful, impatient and confused, whilst our apparently irrational furry friends look on in bemusement, seemingly unfazed by anything (except dogs when the vacuum cleaner is turned on, who proceed to lose all their marbles and go nuts chasing the damn thing around the house until you hit the off switch).

This is none more true than when we are faced with violent confrontation. Our emotions take over and we react to circumstances with fear, self-doubt, insecurity, or on the opposite end of the spectrum, uncontrollable anger and rage.

Your emotions will kill your presence of mind, and thus your ability to react rationally and calmly in a conflict situation.

The more you can maintain your presence of mind in the face of conflict and turmoil, the easier it will be to affect a more favourable outcome to the situation.

As Robert Greene puts it in his must read book, *The 33 Strategies Of War*:

"Understand: your mind is weaker than your emotions. But you become aware of this weakness only in moments of adversity-- precisely the time when you need strength. What best equips you to cope with the heat of battle is neither more knowledge nor more intellect. What makes your mind stronger, and more able to control your emotions, is internal discipline and toughness. No one can teach you this skill; you cannot learn it by reading about it. Like any discipline, it can only come through practice, experience, even a little suffering."

What you need in order to cultivate your presence of mind are exercises of a sort that will provide a counter-balance to the overpowering pull of your emotions.

Presence of mind is needed in all adverse situations, not just in physical conflicts, so when you read the following counter-balance exercises, think about how you can apply these methods to your life as a whole.

Expose Yourself To Conflict

Fear is the most destructive emotion for presence of mind. Given free reign it will decimate whatever presence of mind you have. It thrives on the unknown, which lets our imaginations run wild. It is therefore better to confront your fears and let them come to the surface, rather than ignore them or try to tamp them down.

If you have a major fear of physical conflict then the best way to dampen that fear is to expose yourself to it. No one likes to hear this however, because it means exposing yourself to the very thing that causes you fear.

But expose yourself you must, especially if you want to overcome said fear. Most people have a fear of violence and conflict in general. I did as well, but after so many years of working doors and being exposed to conflicts of one kind or another on a weekly basis, I eventually grew used to it, to the point where I am now able to maintain good presence of mind in such situations. In the beginning I was a total wreck. My presence of mind was often shattered when I had to deal with conflicts or get physical. I thought I would never be as calm and collected as some of the other bouncers I was working with. But eventually I got to that point where I was able to keep my emotions in check, which made it easier for me to deal with situations as they arose.

Exposure therapy is a process. Trust in it and you will eventually get to that place where you want to be.

The sensation of overcoming a deep-rooted fear will in itself give you confidence and presence of mind.

Public speaking was (and still is to an extent) another great fear of mine. As an introvert I found it difficult to speak with confidence to groups of people. Over the years however, I have made a point of putting myself into situations where I have to speak publicly, mostly through instructing classes, and lately to a camera (which is just the same as speaking to a group). My public speaking skills still need work but I'm getting there. Each time I do it, my confidence grows. I have faith in the process.

The more conflicts and difficult situations you put yourself through, the more battle-tested your mind will be.

Start small and go just beyond your comfort zone each time. That's all you have to do. Over time you will make progress and each success will build upon the next.

"There was a fox that had never seen a lion. But one day he happened to meet one of these beasts face to face. On this first occasion he was so terrified that he felt he would die of fear. He encountered him again and this time he was also frightened, but not so much as

the first time. But on the third occasion when he saw him, he actually plucked up the courage to approach him and began to chat."

A fable that shows that familiarity soothes our fears.

Be Self-Reliant

There is not much worse than feeling dependent on other people. Dependency will make you vulnerable to all kinds of negative emotions like betrayal, disappointment and frustration, all of which can play havoc with your presence of mind.

When it comes to your personal safety, self-reliance is even more important. You can't depend on anyone to save you or come to your rescue. You must have the confidence and ability to deal with whatever circumstances you find yourself in.

Going back to my bouncing days, in the beginning I relied quite heavily on the other guys I was working with. If anything happened, I needed their support to deal with things, which didn't really increase my confidence much because I just felt dependant and unable to deal with things by myself. As I became more experienced and my confidence grew however, I learned to stand on my own two feet, and this increased confidence helped me deal with conflicts easier.

Being self-reliant is critical. You need to make yourself less dependent on others, and especially on so-called experts. You can't rely on any instructor or sensei to help you with your personal safety. Placing yourself completely in their hands (as many do) is not the way to go.

Take responsibility and work on expanding your repertoire of skills by yourself. To do this you need to feel more confident in your own judgement.

To quote Robert Greene again:

"Understand: we tend to overestimate other peoples abilities and we tend to underestimate our own. You must compensate for this by trusting yourself more and others less."

Unintimidate Yourself

Feelings of intimidation will always threaten your presence of mind, and it can be a difficult thing to combat. It's kinda hard not to feel intimidated when there is some angry, aggressive individual standing right in front of you who is giving of so much bad intention that you just wish you were somewhere else at that point, far away from the violence that is about to ensue.

Most of these feelings of intimidation are originated by your imagination however. The would-be attacker in front of you may look the part, but that doesn't mean he can act the part as well. Our imaginations give the other guy traits and abilities that they most likely don't even have. You have no way of knowing either way, so why upset your mental balance by thinking about it?

One of the keys to combating intimidation is to see the other guy as just a mere mortal, an ordinary Joe who is about to overstep the mark for whatever reason. See the person, not the myth your mind has probably already created.

Cutting the other guy down to size in this manner will help you to keep your mental balance and presence of mind.

Develop Your Intuition

Presence of mind depends not only on your minds ability to come to your aid in difficult situations, but also on the speed with which this happens.

Speed in this case refers to your ability to respond to circumstances with rapidity and making lightning-quick decisions. This kind of power is often read as a kind of intuition.

In terms of increasing that ability to respond faster to circumstances, there are things you can do to bring out that intuitive feel that all animals possess.

You should first of all have a deep knowledge of the terrain, so to speak. You must understand the nature of the situation you are in and what you have to do. The more you train, the better you get. The more experience you have, the deeper your knowledge of the terrain is going to be.

It will also help to have a good feel for people and a good level of social intelligence. You must know people and their general behaviours, the rituals, the social conventions etc. This will help you predict people's behaviour to a good extent; it will help you understand these kinds of altercations, and it will allow you to spot such situations early, before they develop out of hand.

All of this will give you an intuitive feel for people and situations that will help you in making faster decisions and maintaining your mental balance.

Maintaining Presence Of Mind In Every Day Life

Presence of mind is not just useful in times of adversity. It is not something which you should just switch on and off as you need it. It should be something that you actively try to maintain throughout your daily life. Cultivate it as a daily condition. Work on controlling your emotions and strengthening your internal discipline. Try to maintain a calm and level state of mind throughout your day.

Maintaining presence of mind can prove to be quite difficult at times of course, especially in the face of daily stresses and mental anguish of all kinds. If you find yourself losing your presence of mind, just try to check yourself and bring your mind back around again. It's no big deal. You aren't going to die if you lose your presence of mind so don't beat yourself up about it. Just keep pulling it back into focus when focus is lost.

The better you get at maintaining this mental balance, the more your focused and calm state of mind will do for you in your daily life. When a crisis does come, your mind will already be calm and prepared.

Once presence of mind becomes a habit, it will always remain with you.

APPENDIX C

SOME THINGS YOU SHOULD KNOW ABOUT REAL FIGHTING

1. In a real fight you lose power.

Yes, that's right, you lose power.

You know when you hit the heavy bag in the gym, and you're just laying these hard and heavy shots into the leather and it seems like the bag is about to break free from its chains because you're hitting it with so much power?

Well that doesn't happen much in real combat.

Largely due to the cocktail of stress hormones coursing through your body, you end up losing quite a bit of power.

It makes sense. Turbo charges like that take a lot of energy to produce. A lot of the energy that you normally put into your strikes in practice goes into producing that adrenaline rush. After the initial burst you begin to feel weakened by it.

I've felt this effect and it can come as a bit of a shock when you throw a strike and it feels like you're hitting with a feather. You can't understand why you didn't strike the way you did thousands of times before in training.

That's why. Adrenaline. It has both positive and negative effects. The real key to maximum performance under its influence is knowing what to expect.

So you have to learn about it and you have to experience it first-hand a few times.

When you learn to cope better with the stress reaction, you will also learn to strike more powerfully when in that condition.

A good start to learning to cope would be doing pressure tests and scenario work in the gym. Exposure therapy. What you feel in the gym will not be what you will feel in a real situation exactly, but it'll be enough to get you started. You'll just know to expect more of it.

2. You scrabble in real fights

I know what you're thinking. In a real fight you get an uncontrollable urge to play board games. Something to do with the adrenaline, right?

Not exactly. Although suggesting a game of Scrabble to someone who is about to rip your head off and stare down your neck might be a good ploy to set up a pre-emptive strike, that is not what I mean by scrabble.

Here's the dictionary definition of scrabble:

To scrape or grope about frenetically with the hands.

Yes, that's right. Real violence doesn't tend to play out the way it does in Hard To Kill. Unlike Segal in the movie, you tend not to be that graceful or fluid in a real fight.

Physical confrontations are so hyped up and frantic that it is almost impossible to be graceful, at least not in the way you normally would be when doing techniques in the gym. The adrenaline messes up your co-ordination and fine motor skills a bit.

Hence, you scrabble. You just want to get it over with. You don't have time to be graceful.

That's why real fights always look so scruffy.

Scrabbling.

3. Your ego will often get in the way

You know your ego. It's that asshole who loves himself and is always rudely demanding things; the one who always thinks he's right; the one who can't walk away from a fight, who refuses to turn the other cheek in case they appear weak in the eyes of others.

Think back. In all the times you have had a physical confrontation with someone, how many of those times were at least in part caused by you? How many times could you have easily walked away without recourse to violence?

We've all been in a few bad incidents of our own making, times when we pushed things too far, when we said things out of pride, times when we should have left well alone and walked away.

It was your ego that made you stay when you should have walked, reacted when you shouldn't have, said things you shouldn't have said.

The ego is a powerful force. It has a massively tight grip on most people and its needs are hard to ignore.

It also has a habit of taking over in times of stress.

If you wish to lead a peaceful life then learn to guard against and control your own ego. In a conflict situation it will get you in trouble every time.

It will strive to make you feel bad about doing the right thing. The safest thing.

If some drunk says something rude to your wife your ego will immediately want to reprimand that person. You'll feel like you have to confront the guy, maybe even hit him.

From a self defence point of view that would be the wrong thing to do. Just whatever, the guys a dick, walk away. But your ego will pop up and shout "NO! Hit this dick-now! He insulted your woman!"

I don't need to tell you why that shouldn't happen. Your ego will keep telling you why it should however.

And it's like that in every situation. Unless you have a handle on your sneaky bastard ego it will continue to take over and cause more trouble.

So get a handle on it.

RECOMMENDED RESOURCES

There is a lot of information out there on self defence, between books, videos and the hundreds of websites that exist online. Unfortunately the vast majority of this information is bogus and/or extremely ill-informed. What follows is a small list of resources that I consider to be credible and worth your time.

Books
Facing Violence, by Rory Miller
Dead or Alive, by Geoff Thompson
The Little Black Book of Violence, by Lawrence Kane and Kris Wilder
Combatives for Street Survival, by Kelly McCann

Websites
Combative Mind (www.combativemind.com)
Core Concepts Forum
(www.coreconcepts.forumotion.co.uk)

ABOUT THE AUTHOR

Neal Martin is a personal protection instructor, writer and ex-bouncer. He is also the publisher of the Combative Mind blog. He lives in N.Ireland with his wife and three girls.

Printed in Great Britain
by Amazon.co.uk, Ltd.,
Marston Gate.